Feel
the
Pull

THIRD EDITION

Feel *the* Pull

CREATING *a* CULTURE *of* NURSING EXCELLENCE

Gen Guanci, R.N.

CREATIVE
HEALTH CARE
MANAGEMENT

Softcover ISBN 13: 978-1-886624-74-0
ebook ISBN 13: 978-1-886624-73-3

Printed and bound in the United States.

Second Printing: February 2017

21 20 19 18 17   7 6 5 4 3

CREATIVE

HEALTH CARE

MANAGEMENT

For permission and ordering information, write to:

Creative Health Care Management, Inc.
6200 Baker Road, Suite 200
Minneapolis, MN 55346

chcm@chcm.com or call: 800.728.7766 or
952.854.9015
www.chcm.com

This book is dedicated to my mother,
whose support was never ending.

In addition, it is dedicated to all the individuals
who have the vision and desire to achieve excellence
and who work tirelessly toward that vision.
I have learned from each and every person with
whom I have had the pleasure to partner.

I thank each of you!

CONTENTS

FOREWORD

In *Feel the Pull: Creating a Culture of Nursing Excellence*, Gen Guanci provides a comprehensive guide to understanding the concept of excellence from the perspective of award achievement, as well as the perspective of deep culture change that supports excellent practice.

Although Gen examines excellence through the lens of nursing, the concepts here are entirely applicable to other disciplines in health care as well as other fields. The language is concise, making the book highly readable and free of jargon. Gen uses many real-world situations to make her points throughout the book. Bullet points summarize processes, and simple formulas explain complex concepts. It is a perfect tool for the busy professional or executive.

Gen creates a pragmatic road map for cultural transformation, complete with guides for an organization to follow on the road to excellence. The exploration of organizational assessment is followed by an excellent discussion of how to plan for the change. The discussion of professional practice, empowerment, shared governance, and evidence-based practice is of great value. These areas of practice development are often overlooked and yet are the roots of true excellence in practice.

This book is in sharp contrast to some other approaches to achieving excellence that provide more of a Band-Aid than a cure. Following the process Gen has laid out will enable an organization to achieve deep and lasting culture change that will provide empowered employees with the energy, courage, and will to be innovative and creative caregivers. This book is not a "canned package," full of slogans or catch phrases designed to merely improve scores or achieve better statistics for some report. *Feel the Pull* leads readers on the journey to true excellence in practice.

—Marie Manthey, PhD (hon), MNA, FAAN, FRCN,
President Emeritus, Creative Health Care Management

ACKNOWLEDGMENTS

This book would not be possible without the contributions of the wonderful and passionate team of professionals at Creative Health Care Management. Support, feedback, and encouragement from these professionals played a critical role in the evolution of this book.

My sincere gratitude and profound thanks go to the following individuals:

Chris Bjork, *Resources Director*

Leah Kinnaird, *Peer Reviewer*

Marie Manthey, *Consultant, Foreword Author and Peer Reviewer*

Donna Wright, *Consultant and Peer Reviewer*

James Monroe, *Design and Layout*

Marty Lewis-Hunstiger, *Editor*

Rebecca Smith, *Editor*

I am so proud to have you as my colleagues!

INTRODUCTION

While many individual articles and books have been published about the various excellence awards available in health care, there is a scarcity of materials that look at multiple awards side by side and identify the essentials of a culture of nursing excellence. This book is not a treasure map leading to specific awards. Instead it looks at the common components seen in organizations that have been successful in receiving national recognition for health care and nursing-specific excellence. Whether you are considering pursuing one of these awards, are already on your journey, or are striving to implement a culture of nursing excellence without officially seeking award recognition, this book will become your ongoing reference.

The chapters take you through an overview of several of the awards available in health care today, including the Baldrige Performance Excellence Program Award and the American Nurses Credentialing Center's Magnet Recognition Program®. As you continue through the chapters, you will look at the benefits of creating a culture of nursing excellence, the essentials of this sort of culture, and strategies to facilitate the implementation of the essentials as well as the cultural transformation that inevitably occurs when an organization implements the multifaceted aspects of a culture of nursing excellence.

This book will not walk you through the stages of the application process of any of the awards, nor will it provide step-by-step, how-to instructions. What it will do is stimulate your thinking on what it will take in *your* organization to implement a culture of nursing excellence.

Remember the Five Es

As you progress through the chapters and begin to map out your journey, you would be wise to keep the *Five Es of Nursing Excellence* (Figure I-1) in mind:

1. **Educate:** Educate yourself and your organization on the measures of nursing excellence (award criteria).

2. **Examine:** Conduct a thorough gap assessment.

3. **Essentials:** The essentials are elements of success—the "must haves." Develop your action plan based on the essentials and your gap assessment results.

4. **Empowerment:** Develop programs/processes that support employee involvement and ownership.

5. **Enculturation:** The essentials must become a part of your organization's culture in order to sustain the award-winning environment. (Guanci, 2007)

The tips, suggestions, and tools found in this book are examples of the initiative, innovation, and creativity it takes to successfully build

> *What you get by reaching your destination isn't as important as what you **become** by reaching your destination.*
>
> —AUTHOR UNKNOWN

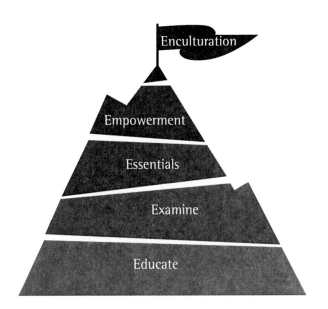

Figure I-1. Five Es of Nursing Excellence (Guanci, 2007).

a culture of nursing excellence regardless of the type of organization. You will see that it is not enough to simply create a culture that is only "skin deep." Total enculturation needs to occur in order for an organization to sustain the true essence of a culture of nursing excellence.

ONE

What is Nursing Excellence?

Nursing excellence can be measured by several factors, the most common being the results of patient satisfaction surveys, especially as they relate to the care patients received. Others include employee engagement or nurse satisfaction surveys, physician satisfaction surveys, and nurse-sensitive quality indicators. Although the results of these measures are primarily for internal use, excellent organizations (including those seeking recognition of their excellence) are utilizing national benchmarks as a point of reference.

So how do you validate your organization's excellence? Many associations and organizations grant recognition and awards that signify excellence. Awards vary from generic (e.g., Best Places to Work) to health care-specific (e.g., Baldrige Performance Excellence Program Award—

Health Care designation) to nursing-specific (e.g., Magnet Recognition Program® designation). While the criteria and categories of evaluation for the awards vary, if you compare awards side by side, you will see common themes emerging. These are the essentials of a culture of excellence.

Before looking at the essentials, a review of some of the major awards available in health care today is warranted. Current awards include:

- Best Places to Work (usually business journal–sponsored, e.g., *Boston Business Journal*'s Best Places to Work award).
- American Association of Critical-Care Nurses (AACN) Beacon Award for Excellence™.
- Baldrige Performance Excellence Program (BPEP) Award (formerly the Malcolm Baldrige National Quality Program Award).
- Individual state-level quality awards.
- American Nurses Credentialing Center (ANCC) Magnet Recognition Program® designation.
- American Nurses Credentialing Center Pathway to Excellence® Program.
- American Nurses Credentialing Center Pathway to Excellence in Long Term Care® Program.

Overview of Select Awards

Best Places to Work

Many local business journals have an annual competition for organizations to be designated a "best place to work." Organizations receiving this designation are those that create positive work environments that attract and retain employees and provide work-life balance. This is accomplished through a variety of programs, including benefits, organizational culture, working conditions, and attention to staff well-being.

The award process is two-pronged, with the organization completing a self-assessment while its employees complete a confidential survey. The employer's questions range from those asking for specifics regarding retirement plans, health insurance, employee education, and other organization benefits to questions regarding vacancy and turnover rates. Employees are asked to answer questions related to rewards and recognition, relationships with their supervisors, potential for career growth, and their favorite things about the organization. Check your local business associations and business journals for further information.

American Association of Critical-Care Nurses Beacon Award for Excellence™ (formerly the Beacon Award)

In 2003, the American Association of Critical-Care Nurses (AACN) established the Beacon Award for Critical Care Excellence. Adult critical-care units, progressive care units, and pediatric critical care units were eligible.

In late 2010, significant program revisions were introduced. These changes include:

- The name was changed to Beacon Award for Excellence.
- The criteria were expanded to allow for application by any unit in which patients receive inpatient care.
- The award duration was extended from one to three years.
- The award was made available at three levels: bronze, silver, and gold.
- The structures and processes were made more congruent with other national awards.
- The evaluation categories were renamed.
- The criteria were linked to nurse-sensitive indicators.

Even though the name may have changed and some of the elements expanded, the purpose of the award did not. The purpose of the award is to:

- Recognize excellence in the inpatient environments in which nurses work and acutely ill patients receive care.
- Recognize excellence of the highest-quality measures, processes, structures, and outcomes based on evidence.

- Recognize excellence in collaboration, communication, and partnerships that support the value of healing and humane environments.

- Develop a program that contributes to the actualization of AACN's mission, vision, and values (AACN, 2011a).

Applicants for the Beacon Award for Excellence are scored in the following five categories, with the maximum score a unit can obtain being 1,000 points.

1. Leadership Structures and Systems: Evaluates the leadership style of the unit as well as support for the professional practice environment. This includes the use of shared decision-making processes and individual accountability. 150 points

2. Appropriate Staffing and Staff Engagement: Looks at staff satisfaction as well as what the unit is doing related to benefits, employee development, and quality of life. 100 points

3. Effective Communication, Knowledge Management, and Best Practices: Includes the types of communication used to ensure continuity and coordination of multidisciplinary care and professional development activities and support, as well as efforts to ensure a healthy work environment. 100 points

4. Evidence-based Practice and Processes: Reviews the unit's use of evidence-based protocols in the development of nursing practice as well as staff access to evidence-based practice resources. In addition, use of best practices is also evaluated. 200 points

5. Patient Outcomes: This, the largest category, looks at the overall outcomes of the unit as well as those related to specific disease processes. An evaluation of the adequacy of staffing is also completed. 450 points

As previously mentioned, three levels of awards were introduced with the 2010 changes. The scores for each level are as follows:

- Bronze Level: Total score 250–400, with the majority of scores at or above the 25% threshold.
- Silver Level: Total score 350–700, with the majority of scores at or above the 50% threshold and few major gaps in any area.
- Gold Level: Total score over 650, with the majority of scores at or above the 70% threshold and no major gaps in any area.

A unit receiving the Beacon Award for Excellence must reapply every three years to maintain its award status. A unit can also reapply earlier if they have implanted systems and processes that they believe would grant them achievement at a higher award level. For further information on the

Beacon Award for Excellence, as well as the self-assessment tool and scoring guidelines, please visit http://www.aacn. org/wd/beaconapps/content/mainpage.pcms.

Baldrige Performance Excellence Program (formerly the Malcolm Baldrige National Quality Program)

Signed into public law by President Ronald Reagan in 1987, the Malcolm Baldrige National Quality Program, renamed the Baldrige Performance Excellence Program (BPEP) in October 2010, is the highest level of recognition an organization can receive for performance excellence. Originally designed for business, there are now five industry-specific awards: manufacturing, service business, small business, education, and health care and nonprofit. Health care is the latest addition, having been added in 1999. Each year there can be up to three winners for each industry-specific award.

In 2015, BPEP unveiled their 2015–16 Baldrige Framework Update changes. Changes include the following:

- A new graphic to represent the criteria.
- Changes to core values.
- Changes to criteria – themes: change management, big data, and climate change.
- Structural changes to overall and multiple requirements.
- Introduction of a new applicant resource: Baldrige Excellence Builder.

Applicants are evaluated in seven performance categories. Weighted scores are given for each category, with the maximum total score being 1,000 points. A minimum score of 500 on the organization's application is required to receive a site visit. Most past recipients have received final scores in the 700 to 800 range. Applicants are evaluated in these categories:

1. Leadership, receiving up to 120 points, looks at how the organization is led, its responsibilities to the public, and how the organization practices good citizenship.

2. Strategic Planning, receiving up to 85 points, evaluates how the organization develops and deploys strategic direction.

3. Customer and Market Focus, receiving up to 85 points, assesses how the organization proactively searches for and establishes sustained relationships with customers.

4. Measurement, Analysis, and Knowledge Management, receiving up to 90 points, assesses how the organization identifies, collects, disseminates, and improves data and knowledge resources.

5. Staff Focus, receiving up to 85 points, reviews how the organization is maximizing the workforce's potential, as well as aligning it with

the organization's mission, vision, philosophy, and strategic plan.

6. Process Management, receiving up to 85 points, examines how the organization develops, deploys, and improves process management. (This category is about process as opposed to results, which is addressed next.)

7. Organizational Performance Results, receiving up to 450 points, or 45% of the total points, indicates loudly and clearly that the BPEP is about results. Not only are the organization's face-value results reviewed, they are benchmarked against those of competitors and other similar organizations (Baldrige, 2015).

In 2002, Sisters of Saint Mary Health Care became the first health care organization to receive the BPEP award, setting the bar high for other health care organizations.

The journey to achieving the BPEP Award is a long one, with past recipients reporting that it often takes six to seven attempts to achieve. Many organizations choose to begin their journey at the local or state level. From its inception in 1987 until November 2014, the BPEP has been awarded to 105 organizations, of which six are repeat recipients. The health care sector has had 19 award recipients. In 2014, 22 organizations from all sectors applied for the BPEP Award. Of these, 12 were health care organizations (National Institute of Standards and Technology

[NIST], 2015). While the overall application numbers dropped in 2012 due to tightening of the eligibility criteria, the number has continued to grow since that time. For further information and self-assessment tools visit http://www.nist.gov/baldrige/.

Individual State-level Quality Awards

Forty-nine states have adopted the BPEP Award criteria and offer state-level quality awards. These awards, most using the same criteria as the national award, are often the first steps for an organization in its quest for the BPEP Award. Organizations use lessons learned and feedback reports from the state-level process as an action plan for their BPEP journey. State-level applications have steadily increased from the initial 111 applicants in 1991, as organizations continue to use the state-level criteria as a path to national BPEP Award designation (NIST, 2015).

American Nurses Credentialing Center Magnet Recognition Program®

During the nursing shortage of the 1980s, several hospitals throughout the United States were attracting and retaining nurses and not feeling the crunch of the shortage. With sponsorship from the American Nurses Association, Margaret McClure and a team of fellow nurse researchers set out to determine what was occurring at those organizations that made them a "magnet" for nurses. Their findings, published in 1983, can be grouped into three categories:

1. Administration, including flexible work schedules, adequate staffing matrixes, and career growth opportunities.

2. Professional Practice, including professional practice models, nurse autonomy, and a positive image of nursing throughout the organization.

3. Professional Development, including customized orientation plans, support for continuing education, and competency-based clinical advancement programs (clinical ladders) (McClure & Hinshaw, 2002).

Several years later, Marlene Kramer and her colleagues began extensive research and a comparison of Magnet and non-Magnet hospitals. Her research identified the following "Essentials of Magnetism":

- Working with nurses who are clinically competent.
- Good RN/MD relationships (collaborative/ collegial).
- Nurse autonomy and accountability.
- Control of nursing practice and the practice environment.
- Supportive nurse manager/supervisor.
- Support for education.
- Adequate nurse staffing.

- Emphasis on concern for the patient (Kramer, 2003).

Others also researched these "Magnet" hospitals and found that overall they had lower morbidity and mortality rates, higher patient and nurse satisfaction, less nurse burnout, and higher levels of nursing professional practice.

In 1993, the American Nurses Credentialing Center (ANCC) established the Magnet Nursing Services Recognition Program for Excellence in Nursing to formally recognize organizations that demonstrated excellence in nursing practice. The early designation process reviewed organizations based on the American Nurses Association's *Scope and Standards for Nurse Administrators* (ANCC, 2000). In 1994, the University of Washington Medical Center in Seattle became the first Magnet-designated facility. Since that time (as of August, 2015), more than 419 hospitals have received or maintained Magnet status. This number, however, continues to comprise less than 6% of the hospitals in the United States.

In 2002, the ANCC, "realizing it requires an initiative on the part of the whole organization and a change in its culture, chose another name—the Magnet Recognition Program®. This change confirmed what nurses already knew and valued . . . "It takes the whole health care team to ensure good patient outcomes" (Guanci, 2005). The program was further revised in 2005 so that the designation review process focused on the 14 Forces of Magnetism®.

The Forces of Magnetism® are "those elements that contributed to an organizational culture that permitted patients to receive excellent care from nurses practicing in an excellent health care environment" (McClure & Hinshaw, 2002, p. 13).

1. Quality of Leadership: Knowledgeable, risk-takers.

2. Organizational Structure: Flat, with unit-based decision-making processes; nursing represented on all executive committees.

3. Management Style: Participative, visible, accessible.

4. Personnel Policies and Programs: Flexible staffing models, staff voice in development of personnel policies and human resource programs, rewards, and recognition; peer review/feedback present.

5. Professional Models of Care: Nurses accountable for practice environment, the coordinators of patient care.

6. Quality of Care: High-quality care an organizational priority, confirmed by outside databases.

7. Quality Improvement: Staff participation in activities that are considered educational.

8. Consultation and Resources: Peer support; knowledgeable experts available and used.

9. Autonomy: Autonomous practice and independent judgment expected; ongoing peer feedback.

10. Community and the Hospital: Strong community presence, long-term involvement.

11. Nurses as Teachers: Teaching incorporated into all aspects of practice.

12. Image of Nurses: Positive, viewed as vital to organizational success.

13. Interdisciplinary Relationships: Positive, mutual respect among disciplines.

14. Professional Development: Valued, strong education presence, career advancement.

In 2008, the ANCC unveiled its new Magnet Model, which, although still built around the original 14 Forces of Magnetism®, comprised five components, all influenced by global issues in health care in general and nursing in particular. This change was a result of a "statistical analysis of final appraisal scores for applications under the 2005 Magnet Recognition Program Application Manual" (ANCC, 2008, p. 22). In August of 2013, the 2014 Magnet Application Manual was released. While there were significant changes related to documentation requirements, the five-component model, portrayed in Figure 1-1, remains the foundational framework. The components are:

1. **Transformational Leadership (TL):** Includes strategic planning, advocacy and influence, visibility, accessibility, and communication.

2. **Structural Empowerment (SE):** Includes professional engagement, commitment to professional development, teaching and role development, commitment to the community, and recognition of nursing.

3. **Exemplary Professional Practice (EP):** The most comprehensive of the components looks at the organization's professional practice model; care delivery system; staffing, scheduling, and budget processes; interdisciplinary care; accountability, competence, and autonomy; ethics, privacy, security, and confidentiality; diversity and workplace advocacy; culture of safety; and quality care monitoring and improvement.

4. **New Knowledge, Innovations, and Improvements (NK):** Looks at research, evidence-based practice, and innovation.

5. **Empirical Outcomes (EO):** Addresses the "so what": what is different as a result of the systems process and infrastructure that are in place (ANCC, 2008).

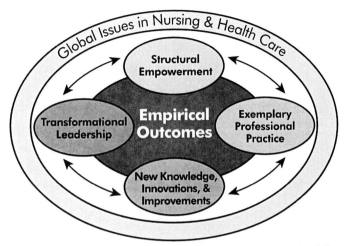

Figure 1-1. The Magnet Model (© 2008 American Nurses Credentialing Center. All rights reserved. Reproduced with the permission of the American Nurses Credentialing Center.)

Figure 1-2 illustrates how the existing 14 Forces of Magnetism® are integrated into the 2008/2014 five-component Magnet Model.

Force of Magnetism®	2008/2014 Magnet Model
Quality of leadership (TL)	Transformational leadership
Organizational structure (SE)	Structural empowerment
Management style (TL)	Transformational leadership
Personnel policies and programs (SE)	Structural empowerment
Professional models of care (EP)	Exemplary professional practice
Quality of care (EO)	Empirical outcomes
Quality improvement (NK)	New knowledge, improvements, and innovation
Consultation and resources (EP)	Exemplary professional practice
Autonomy (EP)	Exemplary professional practice
Community and the hospital (SE)	Structural empowerment
Nurses as teachers (EP)	Exemplary professional practice
Image of nurses (SE)	Structural empowerment
Interdisciplinary relationships (EP)	Exemplary professional practice
Professional development (SE)	Structural empowerment

Figure 1-2. 14 Forces of Magnet Alignment to the 2008 and 2014 Magnet Model (© 2008 American Nurses Credentialing Center. All rights reserved. Reproduced with the permission of the American Nurses Credentialing Center.)

The 2014 manual has 49 Sources of Evidence, 24 of which are outcome focused, that need to be addressed. Organizations that have been successful in receiving Magnet designation state that it takes several years to create, sustain, and enculturate the systems, processes, and infrastructures found in Magnet organizations. Many Magnet organizations say that the journey is all about cultural transformation. For further information, visit http://www.nursecredentialing.org/Magnet.aspx.

American Nurses Credentialing Center (ANCC) Pathway to Excellence® Program and American Nurses Credentialing Center (ANCC) Pathway to Excellence in Long Term Care® Program

The Nurse-Friendly Program, developed by the Texas Nurses Association in 2005, was purchased by the ANCC in 2007 and renamed the Pathway to Excellence (PTE) program. The framework for PTE comprises 12 nurse-authored standards addressing issues that positively influence the work environment:

1. Nurses control the practice of nursing.

2. The work environment is safe and healthy.

3. Systems are in place to address patient care and practice.

4. Orientation prepares new nurses.

5. The chief nursing officer (CNO) is qualified and participates in all levels of the facility.

6. Professional development is provided and utilized.

7. Competitive wages/salaries are in place.

8. Nurses are recognized for achievements.

9. A balanced lifestyle is encouraged.

10. Collaborative interdisciplinary relationships are valued and supported.

11. Nurse managers are competent and accountable.

12. A quality program and evidence-based practices are utilized.

Although the PTE program was originally designed for small organizations (rural, critical access), as well as long-term care and rehab facilities, many organizations are using the program to create work environments that will enable them to be successful in a later Magnet journey. In addition, organizations that are unable to pursue Magnet (e.g., organizations that do not meet Magnet designation requirements for CNOs or nursing leaders) can choose this route.

In 2010, the PTE designation was opened to organizations around the world. Also in 2010, the Pathway to Excellence in Long Term Care® (PTE-LTC) program was launched. PTE-LTC is similar to PTE except the focus is on the unique issues related to long term care environments.

While some may call PTE a "mini Magnet," the ANCC is clear that this is not the case. There are important differences between these programs, including differing application requirements and fees, document submission requirements, verification and validation methods, length of designation, and the degree of focus on outcomes.

TWO

ESSENTIALS OF A CULTURE OF NURSING EXCELLENCE

What do excellent nursing organizations have in common? As you read the criteria and expectations of the awards in the previous chapter, you no doubt identified several recurring themes. These themes are considered the hallmarks of a culture of excellence. They include:

- Strategic planning.
- Stakeholder alignment.
- Staff focus.
- Results/outcomes focus.
- Nurse control over nursing practice.
- Nurse control over the nursing practice environment.

- Rewards and recognition.
- Peer review/feedback.
- Use of evidence-based practice.
- Nursing professional practice.

Whether your organization decides to formally pursue an award or to implement the essentials of a culture of excellence without a formal award pursuit, the cultural transformation and the outcomes associated with such a transformation are priceless.

Benefits to Organizations

Benefits for your organization include:

- Alignment of resources with strategic plans and approaches (e.g., Six Sigma, balanced scorecard, etc.).
- Improved communication, productivity, and effectiveness.
- Recognition of the importance of all employees to organizational success.
- Reinforcement of positive collaborative working relationships.
- Creation of a dynamic and positive environment for all employees.
- Raising of the bar for multidisciplinary patient outcomes.

- Increased marketing advantage.
- Enhanced recruitment and retention of staff and physicians, including:
    - Increased retention and decreased turnover rates.
    - Decreased employee vacancy rates.
    - Decreased time-to-fill rates.
- Decreased morbidity and mortality.
- Increased patient satisfaction.
- Cost savings related to decreased agency use.

In the article "The Business Case for Magnet®," Karen Drenkard states that the range of cost savings that can be achieved for a typical 500-bed organization is estimated at between $2,308,350 and $2,323,350. She goes on to say, "Based upon estimates of direct costs associated with achieving Magnet, which range from $46,000 to $251,000, the potential resulting return on investment is compelling" (Drenkard, 2010, p. 7). Kutney-Lee, Stimpfel, Sloane, Cimiotti, Quinn, and Aiken state, "Magnet recognition is associated with significant improvements over time in the quality of the work environment, and in patient and nurse outcomes that exceed those of non-Magnet hospitals" (Kutney-Lee et al., 2015.)

Benefits Specific to Nursing Staffs

According to current Magnet-designated organizations, their nurses state that a culture of excellence:

- Develops organization/unit pride.
- Promotes an environment with increased teamwork.
- Increases autonomy.
- Increases empowerment.
- Develops a culture of accountability.
- Enhances professionalism.
- Fosters a climate of safety.
- Develops clinical competence of colleagues.
- Decreases burnout.
- Enhances staffing ratios.
- Ensures nursing a voice at the table.

Benefits to Individuals

The last benefits to look at are those to the individual. While many of these have also been identified as either organizational or staff benefits, they deserve repeating. These include:

- Opportunities to develop leadership skills.
- Opportunities to develop and fine-tune mentoring skills.

- Personal satisfaction and recognition.
- Increased career development opportunities.
- Increased sense of professionalism.
- Return of passion for nursing.
- Decreased burnout.
- Increased autonomy.
- Increased empowerment.

Some organizations and individuals will look at the pursuit of excellence and say, "We're already good." To quote Jim Collins, the author of *Good to Great*, "Good is the enemy of great" (2001, p. 1). In *What You Accept Is What You Teach*, author Michael Cohen says that "The pursuit of mediocrity is almost always successful" (2007). The message is clear: If you do not set your expectations high, you will never achieve excellence! Remember what Buzz Lightyear said in *Toy Story*: "To infinity and beyond!" (Pixar Animation Studios & Lasseter, 1995).

THREE

CULTURAL TRANSFORMATION: BRINGING NURSING EXCELLENCE TO LIFE

Organizational culture can be likened to the collective personality of an organization. Culture is the key to what can and cannot survive in any organization and even in an individual department, unit, or shift. The challenge in assessing and determining organizational culture is that culture is unwritten—and often unspoken—and can vary from department to department, unit to unit, shift to shift. Culture develops over time and, once established, remains relatively stable. Furthermore, culture is strongly influenced by the leader(s).

In his book *Organizational Culture and Leadership* (2004), Edgar Schein characterizes culture as having three distinct levels: behaviors and artifacts, beliefs and values, and basic underlying assumptions. An apple can be used to depict these levels (see Figure 3-1). Behaviors and artifacts, the apple's outer skin, are what are visible and include items such as dress code and workplace design. Oftentimes behaviors are performed without employees being able to articulate *why* they are done.

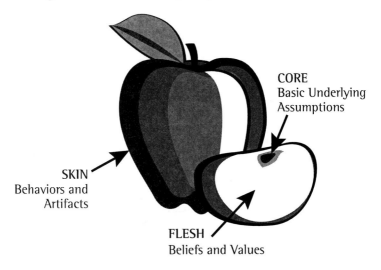

Figure 3-1. The Three Levels of Culture (Guanci, 2007).

Peeling back the skin to show the apple's inner flesh reveals Schein's second level, beliefs and values. These elements are the reasons behind the behaviors and artifacts. In some organizations, there can be a disconnect between stated values and operating values. Asking for employee feedback and opinions and then not acting on or responding to the feedback is an example of this disconnect.

The third cultural level (the apple's core) consists of shared assumptions. Shared assumptions are the by-product of values and beliefs that have been internalized and are then often taken for granted. One example of the effect of shared values and beliefs can be seen in an organization that transitions from an autocratic management style to a shared governance/shared decision-making culture. For years, the employees were not allowed to make any decisions. Now these employees are expected to share not only the decision making but also the responsibility and accountability associated with the decisions. Until the individuals—and the group as a whole—develop trust and new assumptions, they will be slow to embrace the new culture. In fact, they may never be able to embrace the new culture. It is fascinating to interview nurses from organizations that have had shared decision making in place for many years. They have difficulty imagining *not* having shared decision making. This has become their shared assumption. According to Grace, a bedside RN for 19 years, "I don't think I could work at a hospital that did not give me a say in what I do. Who knows better than the nurses doing the bedside work?"

Motivations for Transformation

Factors that influence organizations to transform are many. These may include external restructuring, a new facility or technology, regulatory demands, visionary leadership, a "burning platform" (a need for immediate and radical change due to dire circumstances), or a passion to be better.

Extremely poor patient satisfaction results provided the "burning platform" for Baptist Hospital in Pensacola, Florida. If they were to remain competitive, they needed to undergo a comprehensive organization-wide initiative focused on improving patient satisfaction. Their efforts paid off: Baptist Hospital saw its patient satisfaction scores not only soar but remain among the top in the country. Baptist Hospital is now viewed as a national resource and mentor for other hospitals working to improve their patient satisfaction scores.

Visionary leadership and a passion to be better are among the driving forces behind the growth in the number of award-winning health care organizations throughout the United States. Both the Baldrige Performance Excellence Program and the Magnet Recognition Program® have culture-related requirements, such as risk-taking leaders and a leadership style that includes promotion of autonomy and shared decision making, incorporated into their scoring components.

The Magic of I_2E_2

Jayne Felgen, in her book I_2E_2: *Leading Lasting Change* (2007), describes a change model that she calls I_2E_2 (Figure 3-2). This model begins with a vision and then addresses four distinct elements that must be addressed if change is to be comprehensive and sustainable. Before an organization can even begin to change, it must have a vision. The elements of the model (Inspiration, Infrastructure, Education, and Evaluation) are all interdependent. Inspiration (I_1) requires a shared vision, a collective purpose, and a stimulus for change at all levels. The Infrastructure (I_2) element addresses the development and implementation of the structures, systems, and processes needed to support the desired change. This Infrastructure must include not only the tools but the

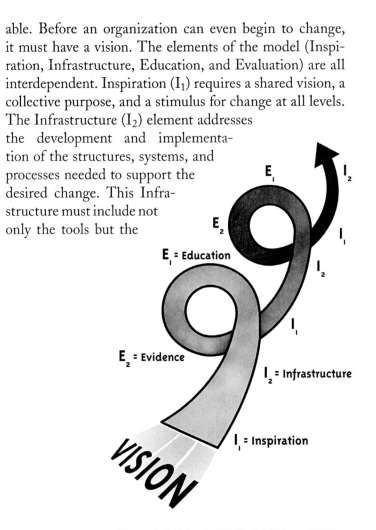

E_1 = Education

E_2 = Evidence

I_2 = Infrastructure

I_1 = Inspiration

Figure 3-2. Felgen's I_2E_2 Model (Felgen, 2007).

continuous and comprehensive communication needed to facilitate change movement. Education (E_1) and the development of a learning environment are required to enable employees to develop the skills and competence required for the change. The final E, Evidence (E_2), addresses the identification of defined and measurable outcomes for the transition. Without measurable outcomes (Evidence that change has occurred), an organization will be unable to validate its success in achieving organizational change.

Unfortunately, many organizations fall short in E_2. New initiatives are developed and rolled out without much thought about how to measure success. The rollout is often followed by a brief, informal evaluation of success, and then it is on to the next initiative. Minimal time and effort are given to sustaining the change. Felgen's I_2E_2 model characterizes lasting change as a continuous and ongoing process, with frequent reinforcement and/or redevelopment of Inspiration, Infrastructure, and Education, all based on Evidence. Working with I_2E_2 helps people to visualize the reality that constantly raising the bar is what is needed to move from a stand-alone, temporary change to sustainable change. Proper implementation of the I_2E_2 model will move your organization from a flavor-of-the-month approach to a true enculturation of the change initiative.

The Four Ps

While planning for change or cultural transformation, your leaders should also consider using a Four Ps approach (Figure 3-3).

Picture:	Where are we now? Where are we going? Where do we want to be?
Purpose:	Why is this needed? Why this change?
Plan:	How do we get there? How will we do this? What is the timeline? Who do we need to involve?
Part:	What is the individual's role in the change? How can he/she help make the change successful?

Figure 3-3. The Four Ps Approach.

The first *P*, Picture, entails communicating to everyone involved in the change initiative a clear picture of "Where are we going?" or "Where do we want to be?" Next, communication related to the Purpose must occur: "Why is this needed? Why *this* change?" The third *P*, Plan, involves communication about "How will we do this? What is the timeline?" Lastly, all employees must be informed of *their* roles or parts in the change, as well as how *they* can help make the change successful. Consistently using this approach has proven to enhance employee engagement.

Proactively identifying and addressing the common mistakes that organizations make when implementing change can help minimize and even eliminate change fiascos. These mistakes can include (1) incomplete and/or infrequent communication; (2) not addressing the Four Ps; (3) lack of trust in the process, leader, or both; (4) lack of shared vision; and (5) lack of accountability. In addition to these mistakes, many organizations quickly move on to the next initiative without taking the time to reflect on what worked and what they must continue to do. Figure 3-4 depicts the continuum of assessment, reassessment, and revisions as needed.

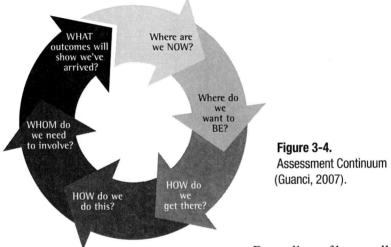

Figure 3-4.
Assessment Continuum (Guanci, 2007).

Regardless of how well planned a culture change is, you must remember that changing a culture is not an overnight process or a "quick fix." Cultural change and transformation can take anywhere from months to years to decades. After all, it is not just the change you are interested in. It is the sustainment or enculturation of the change that is most important. In addition to the enculturation, the change-adept organization is constantly raising the bar and challenging itself to become even better.

FOUR

FINDING THE RIGHT CONSULTANT PARTNER FOR YOUR JOURNEY TO EXCELLENCE

The journey to creating your culture of excellence is a multiyear process, so it is important to decide whether you will go it alone or engage external support. The right consultant can save you significant time, money, and energy as well as potentially play a critical role in the outcomes of your work. Many consultants are worth their weight in gold, while others can do more harm than good. For this reason, it is important to do your homework. Before hiring any consultant—actually before even interviewing anyone—you would be wise to take time to consider all of the information you'll find in this chapter.

Why Use a Consultant for Your Journey?

Perhaps you have had an experience of struggling to learn or do something on your own, only to have someone more skilled or knowledgeable partner with you later. Suddenly things do not seem so overwhelming, confusing, or time-consuming. You find yourself asking why you didn't partner with someone with a higher degree of knowledge or experience sooner. Perhaps you have had the unfortunate experience of spending significant time and money trying to do something on your own, only to be totally unsuccessful, and only *then* turned to an expert for guidance.

Besides bringing expert skill and knowledge, consultants can help you and your organization gain objectivity. This is especially true when it comes to assessing where your organization is in relation to readiness, preparing your written application or document submission, preparing for a site visit, and crafting a "year after plan." An experienced consultant also has a knowledge base that is broad as well as deep. He or she is familiar with your type of excellence journey in a variety of organization types, sizes, and geographical areas. This variety of experience is a critical consideration because you want a partner who is familiar with your type of organization. Such experience with similar organizations will come in particularly handy when searching for examples of evidence to include in your application or document.

If your journey to excellence entails an award or designation process, a skilled consultant can provide focus as well as clarity on award/designation criteria and requirements. Many organizations spend hours trying to develop structures and processes to support their journey to excellence. Consultants often have ready access to vast knowledge of best practices seen through the country. Tapping into that knowledge base can step up the speed of your results.

It is critical that you find a consultant partner who is willing to share his or her expertise and knowledge. Educating and validating key stakeholders in new knowledge and expertise is a major part of a consultant's role and helps instill confidence in those participating in the journey.

Some organizations have hired consultants, not realizing until later that they have made a mistake. Common mistakes in hiring consultants include:

- Making the decision solely on cost.
- Obtaining a full scope of work proposal before an assessment is done. (The consultant's willingness to do this shows potential for lack of customization.)
- Either or both parties being unclear about the scope of work.
- Expecting too much for too little.
- Not checking references.
- Not customizing consultant suggestions to your organization and culture.
- Relying solely on the consultant.

Attention to detail before hiring your consultant will avert most potential problems.

Before Hiring a Consultant

Once you have decided that you do want to hire a consultant, there are many factors to consider as you focus on your end result. Careful deliberation about the multitude of considerations is important because you may be working with your consultant for not just weeks and months but often years. You need to be sure the match is in the best interest of the organization and your desired outcome. Thinking of this phase as the "predating" phase—a time when you decide what you cannot live without and what you are willing to live with—will serve you well.

Decide What Products or Services You Need

There is an old adage that says, "If you don't know where you are going, you will end up somewhere else." The same can be true for not knowing what services or products you will need. Keep in mind that your consultant will also advise you on products and services that will maximize your potential for success. This often occurs after the completion of a readiness assessment (see Chapter Five) or as you work together through the phases of your journey.

The services you may need include some or all of the following:

- General and focused education for a variety of stakeholders.
- Coaching and mentoring of the journey leader.
- Readiness assessment.
- Structure and process development.
- Application and support document review and feedback.
- Electronic document development.
- Site visit preparation.
- Year-after support.
- Redesignation support.

You will also want to consider whether the support you want or need should be done in person or virtually, through conference calls or emails or a combination of both.

Choose Criteria for Selecting a Consultant

Knowing what you want in a consultant is important. Do you want a consultant who comes with an alphabet soup of credentials but limited experience? An individual with lots of experience that is limited to a particular type of organization? Or the individual who costs the least? When considering selection criteria, be sure to look beyond the obvious ones of credentials, services, and experience. Be sure to *ask about* the experiences—how many and what types of organizations. Don't forget to ask about their past results. There is a big difference between the consultant who has worked with 25 organizations, only two of which have gone on to achieve their desired goals and outcomes, and the consultant who has worked with 25 organizations, all of which have reached their desired goals and outcomes.

You should also take into consideration the consultant's availability and accessibility. Is he or she a full-time consultant, or is the consulting work done in addition to another position? It is hard for consultants to be accessible to you when another position consumes the majority of their time.

Other items to consider when choosing among consultants include:

- Do you want a one-person show or a team with expertise in the wide variety of journey components?

- What is their reputation in the specific journey world?

- Who are their references?

- How many repeat clients do they have?

Considering Cost

Hiring a consultant based on cost alone is often an invitation to disaster. "You get what you pay for" is a very true saying when hiring experts. Also remember that a high fee does not equate to being the best. Cost must be taken into consideration, along with the other selection criteria already mentioned, in order to maximize your potential for getting the right consultant for your organization and your specific journey. However, no matter what you decide to pay, cost should be your least important criterion.

How to Find Consultants

Word-of-mouth is a consultant's best advertisement. Clients who are pleased with their consultants are quick to let others know. Social media conversations are a good place to hear about whom to go to and perhaps whom to avoid. Participating in conferences related to the journey you are on is also a great way to meet and/or hear about a variety of consultants, have face-to-face conversations with them, and see examples of their products and services.

Request a Proposal

A business proposal is a written offer from a seller (the consultant) to a prospective buyer. A proposal puts the buyer's requirements in a context that favors the seller's products and services and educates the buyer about the capabilities of the seller in satisfying their needs.

It is important to review the contents of a submitted proposal very carefully because they often give you a glimpse into the quality of work that will be delivered by the consultant. Consider the following proposal elements:

- Does the proposal feel generic? This could indicate that the work delivered will not be customized to your organization.

- Does it articulate the consultant's philosophical beliefs and values, and do these beliefs and values align with your organization?

- Does it feel like the consultant has taken sufficient time to get to know your organization?

- Does it focus on the elements you are requesting?

- Does it feel comprehensive or is it bare-bones?

- Does it focus on the deliverables as well as timeframes?

- Does it quote a lump sum dollar amount or is it based on specific services?

- Does it feel "carved in stone" or is it customized or customizable for your needs?

- Does it include references or other support materials?

- Is it easy to read and understand?

While you may never see a proposal that includes all of these elements, a solid proposal contains many of the best practices listed.

Interview Potential Consultants

Interviewing potential consultants is a critical step in the selection process, yet many organizations do not take the time to ensure that all candidates are interviewed in a similar manner. Many organizations use a team approach in interviewing potential candidates. This team crafts a set of standardized questions, or at least themes, that each candidate will be asked. Be sure to include the following questions:

- How do you stay up-to-date on the specific journey we are interviewing you for?
- How many organizations have you supported?
- How many of these organizations have been successful?
- Do you have experience with our type of organization?
- Do you have experience in initial designation and redesignation?
- Do you use an individual or a team approach?
- Is your consulting based upon personal or second-hand experience?
- What is your philosophical approach to consulting?
- If we ask a past client organization, what will they say are your strengths? What will they say are your opportunities for improvement?

A consultant interview comparison tool will help you keep track of the interview process and enable a quick comparison among the candidates.

Figure 4-1 is a tool you can use to assess the strengths of potential consultant candidates.

Name	Services	Years of Experience	Types of Organizations	Availability
	F = Full journey S&P = Structure and Process E = Education D = Document S = Site visits		A = Acute P = Pediatric C = Cancer R = Rehab I = International O = Other	FT role PT role

Number of Organizations	Type	Approach	Results	Cost	Comments
Number supported	I = Initial R = Redes B = Both	I = Individual T = team			

Figure 4-1. Consultant Interview Comparison Tool.

Final Consideration

The final stage in making your decision is to answer the question, "Does the consultant fit our organizational culture?" This question could prove to be more important than all the other questions you ask. A consultant needs to tailor his or her approach to fit not only the needs of the organization but also its culture (Figure 4-2). Giving attention only to needs, at the expense of culture, could be a disaster in the making.

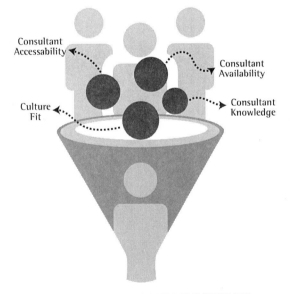

THE RIGHT CONSULTANT PARTNER

Figure 4-2. Finding the Right Consultant Partner.

FIVE

CONDUCTING AN ORGANIZATIONAL READINESS ASSESSMENT OR GAP ANALYSIS AND CREATING YOUR BUDGET

As you read the previous chapters outlining the various categories and components of the American Association of Critical-Care Nurses (AACN) Beacon Award for Excellence™, the Baldrige Performance Excellence Program Award (BPEP), the American Nurses Credentialing Center (ANCC) Magnet Recognition Program® Pathway to Excellence® and Pathway to Excellence in Long Term Care® Programs, you were probably completing a mental checklist. Check, check, check. Got that, need to improve that, need to do that. This mental process is the beginning of your readiness assessment or gap analysis. *Webster's*

New Universal Unabridged Dictionary (2015) defines a *gap* as "an incomplete or deficient area; a problem caused by some disparity."

A readiness assessment looks at where you want to go and what is required to get you there. It compares your desired state with your current state. The items about which you say, "We don't have that" are referred to as *pure gaps*. The items about which you say, "We have some, but . . . " or "We need to improve on . . . " or "We have this in some areas but not all..." are *opportunities for improvement* (*OFIs*). Regardless of whether you have pure gaps or OFIs, they all need to be addressed. Because a thorough, accurate, and unbiased assessment is so important, organizations should strongly consider using an outside resource such as a consultant to ensure an objective assessment. This outside resource must be someone who has experience conducting organizational assessments. He or she must also have thorough knowledge of the specific components and criteria of the award or designation you are pursuing or the essentials you wish to implement. Lastly, he or she must be able to generate a comprehensive written report of his or her findings. Many organizations continue to work with the person or team who conduct their organizational assessment throughout their entire award journey. (Chapter Four has taken you through best practices for hiring a consultant.)

The completed readiness assessment will identify structures, processes, and systems that need to be created and implemented, as well as those that need to be strengthened, and also the cultural changes that must occur in order to move your organization toward its goal. Your organization would be wise to keep in mind that it will take much more time to change a culture than to implement structures, processes, or systems. Most agree that it takes anywhere from one to nine years to change a culture (never mind sustaining the culture change).

One mistake many organizations make when conducting a readiness assessment is to do a fine job completing the assessment at the organizational level, but the drill-down to the department and, more specifically, to the unit level, never occurs. One example may be when an organization with a well-established nursing division practice council operates under the principles of shared governance but lacks unit-level councils or has unit-level councils on only a few of its nursing units. The organization has a deficit that must be addressed.

Award Grantor Readiness Assessmements

In order to help an organization determine its readiness to pursue a specific award, most grantors of awards have created readiness assessments. One tool found on the ANCC PTE website is the Pathway to Excellence® Organizational Self-Assessment. This tool is a survey asking a series of questions that support the PTE standards, such as, "Does the organization promote and encourage self-care for nurses on the job?" This tool is a great way to introduce the various components of the PTE Program to your organization's nursing workforce.

In addition to the PTE tool, you can find the *Organizational Self-Assessment for Pathway to Excellence in Long Term Care*® tool on the ANCC website.

The Baldrige Performance Excellence Program has several tools for public use. One tool, *Baldrige Self-Assessment and Action Planning*, is described as "a snapshot of your organization, the key influences on how you operate, and the key challenges you face" (NIST, 2015). The first section of the tool, *Organizational Description*, addresses your organization's health care environment and your key relationships with patients, customers, suppliers, and other partners.

The second section, *Organizational Challenges*, calls for a description of your organization's competitive environment, your key strategic challenges, and your system for performance improvement. If you identify topics for which, little, no, or conflicting information is available, it is possible that your assessment need go no further, and you can use these topics for action planning. Of the remaining tools, one is a staff-focused self-assessment, *Are We Making Progress?* (NIST, 2011a); one is a leader-focused self-assessment, *Are We Making Progress as Leaders?* (NIST, 2011b); and one is the *Baldrige Excellence Builder* (NIST, 2015). Completing a variety of tools helps an organization identify its pure gaps and OFIs and will often be the first identification of any disconnect between executive management, other leaders, and staff.

The AACN Beacon Award for Excellence also has an audit tool available for public use on its Beacon Award for Excellence website (AACN, 2015). Regardless of the award you are pursuing, you should employ an organized approach to your readiness assessment and the subsequent action plan. One method is to create a document that lists the specific components (the sources of evidence that meet the requirements) and the status of the sources of evidence. Some organizations also find it helpful to use this same readiness assessment document as their action planning tool. By adding a section on who is responsible for each component and/or source, as well as the required timeline, everyone can see the big picture (see Figure 5-1). Not only will you have a measure of where you are and where you need to go, you will have a measure of how far you have come. It is this how-far-you-have-come measurement that will help raise the spirits of all involved during the inevitable times of self-doubt.

Sample Gap Assessment Tool

COMPONENT	DESCRIPTION	GAP	SOURCE OF EVIDENCE	PERSON(S) RESPONSIBLE	STATUS
TL	*Transformational Leadership*				
	Strategic Planning: Describe and Demonstrate				
TL1EO	Nursing's mission, vision, values, and strategic plan align with the organization's priorities to improve the organization's performance.	No	Employer of choice goals: Decreased vacancy rates, decreased retention, improved RN satisfaction.		

COMPONENT	DESCRIPTION	GAP	SOURCE OF EVIDENCE	PERSON(S) RESPONSIBLE	STATUS
TL	*Transformational Leadership*				
TL2	Nurse leaders and clinical nurses advocate for resources to support unit and organizational goals.	No	Sim. lab funding request from education. Request for additional COWs [computers on wheels] for Med/Surg units.		
TL3	Strategic planning structure(s) and process(es) used by nursing to improve the health care system's effectiveness and efficiency.	No	Orientation, charge nurse, and preceptor programs, leadership development forums, and CE programs.		
Advocacy and Influence: Describe and Demonstrate					
TL3EO	Outcome(s) that resulted from the planning described in TL3.	Yes	Smoke-free program outcomes. Outcomes of the Adopt-a-Unit program. No pre- or postmeasures available.		
TL4	The CNO is a strategic partner in the organization's decision making.	No	Board member, EPIC		

COMPONENT	DESCRIPTION	GAP	SOURCE OF EVIDENCE	PERSON(S) RESPONSIBLE	STATUS
TL	*Transformational Leadership*				
TL4EO	One (1) CNO-influenced organization-wide change.	Yes	Smoke-free program outcomes. Outcomes of the Adopt-a-Unit program. We do not measure these at this time.		
TL5	Nurse leaders lead effectively through change.	No	Water main break. Unplanned LOA of both Director of Med/Surg and Maternal/Child.		
TL6	The CNO advocates for organizational support of ongoing leadership development for all nurses, with a focus on mentoring and succession planning. Mentoring and/or succession planning for: Leadership development. Performance management. Mentoring activities. Succession planning for nurse leaders.	OFI All 4 types	Need to create a nursing succession plan that includes leadership development and a formal mentoring program for emerging leaders.		
TL7	Nurse leaders, with clinical nurse input, use trended data to acquire necessary resources to support the care delivery system(s).	Yes	Staff unable to speak to care delivery system as it has been neither declared nor developed.		

Figure 5-1. Sample Gap Assessment Tool (Guanci, 2007, revised 2013).

Whatever approach you choose to take with your organization's readiness assessment, you must remember that it will determine the road map for your journey, so it is essential that you take time to ensure that the assessment is done thoroughly and accurately. If you fail to do so, you will end up spending precious time trying to get back on the road. Worse yet, you may never arrive at your destination. See Figure 5-2.

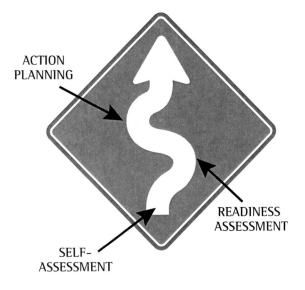

ACTION
PLANNING

READINESS
ASSESSMENT

SELF–
ASSESSMENT

Figure 5-2. Readiness on the Journey to Excellence (Guanci, 2007).

Creating Your Budget

The journey to excellence requires careful consideration of the budget. These costs must be included in the initial development of the annual budget, not just "added costs" incorporated into the already developed current budget. Consideration must also be given to the fact that these costs will continue for several years. Many, if not most, of the costs will remain after an organization reaches its excellence destination. Many organizations underestimate the cost of their journey, so be sure to allow adequate time for brainstorming all the potential costs associated with your journey. Costs to consider include:

- Initial education costs.
- Assessment fees.
- Award fees.
- External consultant fees.
- Human resources costs.
- Costs of implementation.
- Costs of documents and educational materials.
- Marketing costs.
- Celebration costs.
- Award/designation sustainment costs.

Initial Education Costs

To make an informed decision to move forward on an award or designation quest, your organization's decision-makers must be knowledgeable about what it will take to reach your goal. The costs for participation in local, regional, and national award-specific education programs must be budgeted for (e.g., registration, travel, etc.). Additionally, site visits to award-winning organizations provide a learning experience that should not be missed—and therefore should also be included in the budget.

Organizational Assessment/Readiness Assessment Fees

Should this assessment be completed internally or by an external consultant? Organizations that have gone through a designation or award process will confirm the added value of an external resource. Ask yourself: Do you have the expertise, time, and assessment experience to complete the readiness assessment internally, or will it be more cost-effective in the long run to employ the resources of an external consultant? Also, does your organization's culture not want to hear less than perfect feedback from those who work there? If so, you will need honest feedback from an external individual. Another possibility is that *you* see what needs to be done, but others do not agree with you. If you work in an organization in which you would be seen as a "prophet without honor in your own land," you will probably need the assistance of an external consultant. Regardless of your reason, the completion of a readiness assessment and the subsequent assessment report will be a road map for your journey.

Award Fees

Included in this group are the fees associated with the initial application, off-site appraiser/reviewer fees, and appraiser/review team site visits. Many times the total award fees depend on the size of your organization: the larger your organization, the higher the award fees.

External Consultant Fees

As previously mentioned, your organization needs to decide whether to engage an experienced external consultant. This decision should take into consideration your organization's potential costs associated with time, the availability of internal human resources, and the ability of these human resources to move the process forward in an organized, timely manner. If your organization does decide to use an external consultant, you can control how much or how little involvement the consultant has in your journey. The services the consultant offers can vary. Most will offer support in developing the structures and processes needed for successfully achieving the award or designation, the mentoring and coaching of key personnel in the interpretation and development of submission documentation, and site visit preparation. Refer to Chapter Four for guidelines for choosing a consultant partner.

Human Resources Costs

Consideration must be given to the human resources needed to support the program/journey. These include an experienced program manager, as well as the administrative support individuals needed to support the systems, processes, and structures implemented as part of your award quest. Often organizations believe that their program manager must be an individual who has been through the process before. This can sometimes be an asset and sometimes a liability. The person may have experience with the program from the organization in which they used to work, but does he or she know how to operationalize it in your organization's culture?

Costs of Implementing Systems, Processes, and Structures Identified During Your Readiness Assessment

Your readiness assessment identifies what systems, processes, and structures you will need to budget for. These could include capital equipment, unit-specific resources, and information technology resources (e.g., more computers so that nurses have ready access to online sources of best practice guidelines), as well as nonproductive time for staff to participate in the systems and processes (e.g., councils). Lastly, do not overlook monies for staff education to support your new systems, processes, and infrastructures.

Costs of Creating and Preparing Documents and Educational Materials

This budget item should include the costs associated with required documentation. Most award grantors require several copies of your support documentation, and many require that this documentation be bound. Additional costs include those associated with internal materials used for educational and informational purposes. In an effort to support "Green Initiatives," many award and designation grantors are transitioning to electronic documents, including submission online or on flash drives. If you chose this format, there will be additional costs to have the electronic document formatted so that it meets all the requirements of the grantor. Fees associated with electronic documents vary greatly, as does the quality, so shop around to find a solution that fits your needs. (Refer to Appendix B for questions to ask yourself about an electronic self-assessment document.)

Marketing Costs

Your marketing costs must include the costs incurred before, during, and after the award journey. How will you market the process and outcome to your staff, stakeholders, patients, and community? Several grantors require public notices to be posted in more than one format prior to site visits. This format could include newspaper ads, social media, posters placed throughout your organization, and even radio and TV spots. Consideration should also be given to the costs associated with how you will let everyone know of your success.

Celebration Costs

This line item includes the costs associated with receiving your desired award or designation and the celebration that follows. Consideration should also be given to additional celebrations along the journey in order to help maintain momentum. There are several milestones throughout an award journey that welcome a celebration: when you send in your documentation, when you complete your site visit, or even in the middle of a bleak winter when your staff is feeling stressed. Celebration costs could include amenities such as food, giveaways, decorations, photos, and the like.

Award/Designation Sustainment Costs

Many organizations overlook the costs associated with maintaining and sustaining their award or designation. A good general rule to operate under is that all the previously budgeted costs will continue throughout the life of your award. When reapplying for your award, most grantors require that you show verification that you have not only sustained your award status but have raised the bar—which often adds additional costs. Don't forget to budget for the completion of a vulnerabilities assessment that will help identify risk areas that could be based upon changes in the award or designation program.

Just like when you're renovating a home, keep in mind that things often cost more and take longer to implement than originally thought, so plan accordingly. Using the home renovation suggestion of adding 15–20% to what you think you need, both in terms of time and dollars, is a good practice to adopt.

Other Activities

You've completed your organizational assessment and created your budget, so what else can you do to get started on your journey to nursing excellence? Award-winning organizations agree that site visits to organizations that have achieved what you are aiming for are an invaluable undertaking. Locate award winners in your area, and arrange visits with as many as possible. Do not limit yourself to the "biggest and best," and be sure to include organizations that are similar to yours. If you are a small rural hospital, visiting a large academic medical center will still be beneficial, but you may have a hard time convincing your site visit participants that your organization can achieve what the large medical center achieved. Involving staff in site visits is extremely worthwhile. The host organization's staff will be able to share their experience with their guest colleagues and advocate for the pursuit of nursing excellence. In turn, those who attend the site visit will be able to share their experiences and observations with their colleagues once they return. The voice of the staff who went on the site visit will foster a we-are-all-on-this-journey-together mindset, as opposed to they-[the nursing administration]-want-this.

While on the site visits, you may find that you form a special connection with a particular organization. The BPEP Award and the Magnet Program have expectations that successful organizations will mentor those pursuing the recognition. Many individuals from award-winning organizations eagerly serve as mentors for aspiring organizations. Seize this opportunity. Dozens, if not hundreds, of questions will arise over the course of your journey. Your mentor has been through the process and more than likely found answers to these same questions. The camaraderie, suggestions, guidelines, tips, and how-to's you will gain from this mentorship are priceless!

Other options to increase your knowledge include participation on award-specific electronic mailing lists and support groups, as well as attendance at conferences. Ask colleagues about award-specific support groups available in your geographical area. While on your site visits, ask the organizations which electronic mailing lists or groups they have found to be particularly beneficial, and join them.

Most award grantors host regional and national workshops that can increase your knowledge of a specific award. The BPEP and the ANCC conduct annual conferences entitled Quest for Excellence and the National Magnet Conference, respectively. In addition, they host many regional sessions. The award grantors' websites (such as http://www.nist.gov/baldrige/ and http://www.nursecredentialing.org/Magnet.aspx/) provide access to a host of support materials to assist you on your journey.

SIX

STRATEGIC PLANNING
AND STAKEHOLDER ALIGNMENT

Strategic planning, while common practice in business circles, is a relatively new concept for some nursing departments. Organizations have long had annual corporate goals, strategies, and plans; however, it is a current expectation that nursing departments, and even individual nursing units, develop strategic plans that relate to the overall organization plan. A strategic plan is "proactive, vision-directed, action oriented, creative, innovative, and oriented toward change" (Yoder-Wise, 1999). It answers the questions:

- Where are we?
- What do we have to work with?
- Where do we want to be?

- How do we get there?

Strategic planners agree that comprehensive plans follow a prescribed format:

- Completion of an environmental assessment.
- Completion of an assessment of strengths, weaknesses, opportunities, and threats (SWOT; see Figure 6-1).
- Development of specific, measurable, action-oriented, realistic, timed goals (SMART goals; see Figure 6-2).
- Development of an action plan (strategies to meet goals).
- Implementation of strategies.
- Evaluation of progress toward goals.

Environmental Assessment

The environmental assessment is a two-step process that answers the first two questions of strategic planning: "Where are we?" and "What do we have to work with?" To answer these questions, a review of external as well as internal factors and drivers must be completed. The external assessment includes issues such as geographical impact, demographic impact, competition, and political issues, whereas the internal assessment looks at items such as the physical plant, human resources, financial stability, and resources as well as current programs and processes.

SWOT Assessment

Like the internal environmental assessment, a SWOT assessment answers the question, "What do we have to work with?" The organization's SWOT can be divided into internal aspects (strengths and weaknesses) and external aspects (opportunities and threats). Some organizations choose to divide their SWOT into positive aspects (strengths and opportunities) and negative aspects (weaknesses and threats). Remember to include in your strategic plan how you will deal with the challenges identified in your SWOT. Figure 6-1 shows one example of a SWOT:

Strengths
Weaknesses
Opportunities
Threats

Figure 6-1. SWOT Analysis

- **S***trengths:* Committed, hard-working long-term employees.

- **W***eaknesses:* A culture of low accountability; absence of acceptance of responsibility.

- **O***pportunities:* No other award winners in the state.

- **T***hreats:* Organization rushes from one project to another without thoroughly evaluating or sustaining outcomes of prior projects.

Specific
Measurable
Action-oriented
Realistic
Timed

Figure 6-2. SMART Goals

Setting SMART Goals

Goal setting is the critical component of strategic planning that answers the question, "Where do we want to be?" By following the acronym SMART, you ensure that your goals are well developed, with an intended/desired target and an identifiable end point. See Figure 6-2.

- **S***pecific:* Something you want.
- **M***easurable:* How much, how many?
- **A***ction oriented:* How will you get what you want?
- **R***ealistic:* Within your control.
- **T***imed:* When will you reach the goal?

Here is an example of a goal in need of improvement:
Teach a class on Moderate Conscious Sedation.

Here is the same goal, written as a SMART goal:
Work with the Emergency Department (ED) Clinical Nurse Specialist (CNS) to develop and teach a one-hour Conscious Sedation class in the Spring ED Novice Nurses

program.

Developing an Action Plan

An action plan provides the tactics or strategies needed to reach a goal. The organizational readiness assessment sets the direction for the organization's action plan. It is the road map to the destination, not how to reach the destination. Using the SMART goal example identified earlier, the associated action plan might look like this:

- Schedule appointment with ED CNS to discuss project.

- Independently develop measurable, learner-focused program objectives.

- Independently develop presentation outline.

- Review objectives and outline with ED CNS and revise as indicated.

- Develop session presentation for staff nurse participants.

- Develop session handouts for staff nurse participants.

- Review session presentation and handouts with ED CNS.

- Revise session presentation and handouts as indicated.

- Conduct education session for staff nurse participants.

- Evaluate session using a five-point Likert scale.
- Revise program as needed.

If you were developing an action plan for your award journey, some action steps would include:

- Hiring or identifying a program director/ coordinator for the specific award.
- Creating a program budget.
- Identifying program steering committee members.
- Developing a timeline.
- Conducting education sessions for key stakeholders.
- Developing action plans for pure gaps.
- Developing action plans for OFIs.
- Identifying documentation creation teams.

These action plans may seem simple and the details obvious. However, for many organizations, the details of the plan are what is needed to stay on track and keep moving forward. This is especially true in organizations in which there are multiple high-priority initiatives, those that lean toward reactive approaches as opposed to proactive approaches, and/or those going through transitions. Remember, every detail matters!

Stakeholder Alignment

A *stakeholder* is any person or entity who has an interest in the activity, goal, or outcome. Stakeholders for an award journey could include the board of trustees, executive management, leadership team, employees, and physicians. Every stakeholder must understand his or her role in the journey. Roles could include finance approval, responsibility for the implementation of systems and processes, or collecting data measuring progress toward the goal. A clear understanding of the goals, individual roles, and measurable outcomes must be articulated by every stakeholder to ensure that everyone is on board. Only when this is accomplished can you begin to move the entire team toward the desired goal.

Everyday Strategic Planning

Every day we engage in strategic planning and key stakeholder alignment in one form or another. "Not me," you say? Let's take the scenario of planning a daughter's wedding. When she became engaged, the strategic planning

> *"A goal without a plan is just a wish."*
> —ANTOINE DE SAINT-EXUPÉRY, FRENCH WRITER (1900–1944)

process was set into motion. First an assessment of the external and internal environments began. The external environment assessment included these typical questions:

- Who else is getting married and when?

- Will the venue for the wedding and reception be available on the desired date?
- What is the typical weather at that time of the year?
- Are the desired flowers available at that time of the year?

At the same time, an internal environmental assessment is occurring:

- Will both sets of families be available at the proposed time of year?
- Will they approve of the venue?
- What type of wedding can we afford?
- Who will be in the wedding party?
- What type of bridesmaid dress will work for everyone—including Suzy, who will be nine months pregnant by that time?

You may think the goal for the scenario is pretty obvious, yet it needs to be clearly defined. Is the goal simply that Mary and John will get married? Or should it be a SMART goal—that Mary and John will be married in St. Francis Church, at 2 p.m. on June 9, by Father O'Toole? Once you clarify the goal, then the planning begins. (In this case, some of the planning may well have started when Mary was a little girl!)

The action planning for a wedding is so detailed that an entire industry has developed around it. Magazines, wedding planners, and bridal shows abound to help those less familiar with the details of a wedding. As the date draws closer, various strategies of the action plan are implemented, such as buying the dress, getting the dress altered, choosing the reception location, and sending invitations. Simultaneously with the implementation, the mother of the bride and the bride-to-be are conducting an ongoing evaluation of progress toward the goals and making adjustments to ensure that everything will be ready for the wedding.

No matter what type of plan you are developing, here are six things to remember:

1. Align your plan with the organization's overall plan.

2. Identify your key stakeholders.

3. Communicate your plan to all stakeholders.

4. Articulate your expectations.

5. Share the responsibility and accountability for attainment of goals.

6. Provide periodic written progress reports.

SEVEN

WHAT IS NURSING PROFESSIONAL PRACTICE?

We have heard over and over that nursing is a profession. But what is it that makes it a profession? Is it our education? Is it our numbers? Is it the fact that we carry a license?

All will agree that no one factor, or tenet, makes a profession. It is a combination of several tenets that include:

- A well-defined body of knowledge.
- A code of ethics.
- Continuing education.
- A depth of education.
- Control over practice and the practice environment.

- Self-regulation.
- Use of evidence-based practice and research.
- Peer review.
- The ability to practice autonomously.
- Affiliation with professional organizations.
- A system of values.

And in the case of nursing, a primary tenet of the profession is the development of a unique relationship with the patient. Notice that *caring* and *compassion* are not listed as tenets of nursing professional practice. This is because while caring is the essence of nursing practice, caring alone does not make one a professional. The public knows that nursing is a "caring profession," but it is doubtful that they know what it takes to care for a patient. Suzanne Gordon, author of *From Silence to Voice: What Nurses Know and Must Communicate to the Public* (2002), states, "Nurses know that they can and do act on clinical judgment. Now they need to tell the public this." Barbara Blakeney, former American Nurses Association (ANA) president, states, "Nurses do an excellent job of talking about caring and compassion; we present ourselves to the public as people who care—but our failure is that we do not talk enough about the knowledge that backs up the work we do, the reasons why we do those things, and how much we have to know to do them safely." We need to proactively address the challenges facing the future of our profession as an intellectual discipline.

Body of Knowledge/Depth of Education

Nursing has struggled for years with the inability, or unwillingness, to define the entry-level education requirement to become a nurse. Today, we have a cafeteria menu of educational choices: diploma, associate degree (ADN), baccalaureate degree (BSN or BAN), master's degree (MSN), doctor of nursing practice (DNP), and nursing degree completion programs for individuals who have a bachelor's or master's degree in a field other than nursing. In no other profession are there so many entry-level choices. In 1965, the first ANA position paper on the subject called for the BSN as the minimum requirement for entry into nursing (ANA, 1965). Yet more than five decades later, only one state had changed its nurse practice act to reflect the ANA's position. North Dakota, in 1987, added this requirement to its state nurse practice act. (In 2003, public pressure led to the reversal of this change.)

In 2010, the Institute of Medicine (IOM) issued a report, *The Future of Nursing: Leading Change, Advancing Health*. The report contains a series of recommendations, including the following related to BSN level education: "Increase the proportion of nurses with a baccalaureate degree to 80% by 2020" (IOM, 2010, p. 3).

In addition, professional organizations such as the American Organization of Nurse Executives (AONE), as well as specialty organizations such as the National Association of Neonatal Nurses (NANN), have published statements in support of the ANA position paper.

A review of all health care professions finds that entry-level nurses have the lowest level of education. Occupational therapy (OT), physical therapy (PT), and pharmacy all have raised their entry-level requirement to a doctoral degree. In some health care specialties, aides or assistants, such as PT and OT aides, are educated at the associate degree level.

Aikens and colleagues at the University of Pennsylvania whose research study, *Educational Levels of Hospital Nurses and Surgical Patient Mortality* (Aiken, Clarke, Cheung, Sloane, & Silber, 2003), compared the three types of basic nursing education programs (RN diploma, associate degree, and baccalaureate) and found a significant relationship between the education of nurses and patient deaths: "Our findings indicate that surgical patients cared for in hospitals in which higher proportions of direct care RNs held bachelor's degrees experienced a substantial survival advantage over those treated in hospitals in which fewer staff nurses had bachelor's or higher degrees" (Atkins et al., 2003). The 2010 Carnegie Foundation Report calls for radical transformation in the current structure for educating nurses (Benner, 2010).

The double-edged news is that the issue of entry-level education requirements has not gone away, as many current nurse opponents had hoped. The exasperating news is that we as a profession have missed several "deadlines." In 1978, the ANA issued a resolution that "by 1985 the baccalaureate degree would be the required minimum preparation" (ANA, 1978a). In 1982, the ANA again reaffirmed this position. Yet with the initial target date of 1985 looming and no significant progress toward adoption of the resolution by the various states, the ANA issued a new target date of 1995. Unfortunately, that date also came and went. The most recent ANA target for the BSN as the required entry-level education was 2010 (Barter & McFarland, 2001). That too has been missed. Currently 21 states are considering the adoption of "BSN in 10" legislation requiring future registered professional nurses to earn a BSN within 10 years of initial licensure in order to maintain their licensure. The New York legislature has pondered this legislation on eight separate occasions. If this change to entry-level education requirements is to come to fruition throughout the nursing profession, much work remains to be done!

What has helped move the nursing workforce toward the IOM's "80% by 2020" recommendation are the many organizations that have earned or are aspiring to Magnet designation. According to data published on the ANCC Magnet website in February 2014, 55.56% of clinical nurses hold a BSN or higher; in pediatric facilities, the proportion is 70.28% (ANCC, 2014).

Current Magnet hospitals, as well as those that are on the journey, must describe and demonstrate that they have action plans in place to move toward the IOM recommendations. Many organizations seeking excellence have created on-site RN-to-BSN and/or RN-to-MSN programs. Additionally, many organizations have implemented financial support initiatives that go beyond simple tuition reimbursement for employees wishing to obtain a BSN. Several award grantors look favorably on these types of programs as an indicator of a hospital's investment in their employees.

Certification

National certification also plays a role in the identification of a well-defined and deep body of knowledge. Nurses should be encouraged to obtain certification within their area of specialization. According to the ANCC, certification builds confidence in your professional ability, demonstrates that you meet national standards, and validates your nursing knowledge. It shows dedication to nursing as a profession (ANCC, 2007b).

One of the major barriers to obtaining specialty certification is fear—fear of failure, fear of not knowing where to start, fear of doing it alone. The following messages were among those written by nurses at the American Association of Critical-Care Nurses' 2006 National Teaching Institute (NTI) Certification Celebration to encourage nurses considering certification (Briggs, Brown, Kesten, & Heath, 2006). Postcards with the handwritten messages are now being included in exam handbooks and other certification preparation materials:

Dear Future Certified Nurse, I want to encourage you to study, sit for, and pass your certification exam. You will be so glad you did. While I dreaded opening those books again, once I started learning it made my job so exciting. I had so many "ah ha!" moments where I connected what I did on a daily basis to why I did it and why it worked. This exam validates what you already know and already do as second nature. It is hard, and you have to study, but it is worth it. Come join a powerful voice in health care.

★ ★ ★

A certified nurse inspired me to take the exam. I had been on the fence and hesitated taking the exam, even though I had accumulated books and review materials, and had attended seminars for six years. This nurse said to me "What's the worst that can happen if you don't pass? Nothing. What's the best thing? You validate your incredible knowledge and skills. Get on with it." And I did. You can too!

★ ★ ★

I was where you are; you already know you care, you already know you're a great nurse. Prove to yourself and others you can take it a step further and become certified!

★ ★ ★

You have the courage and knowledge within you. Reach for your dream without fear of failure, but with the vision of satisfaction as you achieve your dream and become a better care provider. JUST DO IT!! (AACN, 2006)

If your organization wishes to achieve excellence, you would be wise to consider programs that encourage and support certification endeavors. Many organizations reimburse costs only after the candidate achieves certification. For many nurses, the initial outlay of the $200–$400 exam fee is a deal breaker. They cannot afford to pay this fee hoping they will pass the exam and then receive reimbursement only if they pass. The organizations that excel at excellence are the ones that are willing to invest in their employees and pay the exam fee up front. These same organizations do not require repayment in the event that the candidate is not successful. This sends a powerful message to the employee: We value you, we are willing to take risks, and we will support you in this endeavor regardless of the outcome.

The ANCC, as well as the Pediatric Nurses Certification Board (PNCB), have launched programs to support organizations as they encourage nurses to attain certifications. These programs remove the need for upfront exam fees. For further information on the ANCC Success Pays™ program, visit http://www.nursecredentialing.org/SuccessPays. For further information on the PNCB No Pass No Pay program, visit http://www.pncb.org/ptistore/control/np/index.

Other approaches to increasing nurses' interest in certification include financial support for review courses, hosting on-site review courses, and even conducting homegrown study groups. While on their Magnet journey, one organization took this study group approach when 11 members of their nursing leadership team decided to sit for the ANCC Certified Nursing Administrator (CNA) exam (now called the Certified Nurse Executive [CNE] exam). The group made a considerable time commitment, meeting for one hour every week for 20 weeks. The study group was educator-facilitated and participant-led, with each leader taking responsibility for the review of two or three topics. The organization paid for review books for each participant as well as the up-front cost of the exam. It even supported the group with a hypnosis session to reduce test anxiety! The organization's support paid off: 100% of the nursing leaders attained their certification on the first attempt. This was then highlighted in their Magnet application documents and was commented on by their Magnet appraisers during the site visit. Similar to programs that support nurses attaining their BSN, many award grantors look favorably on programs that support professional certification. Indeed, the ANCC Magnet Program's demographic profile requires organizations to submit the number of certified nurses they employ as well as their plans and goals for increasing this number. The current Magnet facility average for certification for both nursing leaders and clinical nurses is 62.66% in acute care facilities and 74.41% in pediatric facilities (ANCC, 2014).

Continuing Education

Most professions have a continuing education requirement in order to maintain licensure. Nursing, however, has failed to reach consensus on required continuing education requirements. Many states have implemented continuing education requirements, with the amount of education varying from state to state. Of the 36 states that require continuing education (Figure 7-1), the amount varies from as few as 5 hours to a maximum of 36 hours per licensure period. Some states, such as Florida, New York, and Oregon, require education in specific areas such as domestic violence and infection control. Organizations that have a culture of excellence often implement their own continuing education expectations, often as a requirement in their clinical advancement program. These continuing education programs frequently include staff in developing and presenting topics, giving individuals the opportunity to develop their presentation skills and share expertise. However, it is not the required education that is the hallmark of a professional. It is the constant striving for self-improvement, the desire to learn, the desire to explore new horizons, and the desire to share expertise with others who support nursing as a profession.

Florence Nightingale said it succinctly: "Unless we are making progress in our nursing every year, every month, every week, take my word for it we are going back" (Nightingale, 1860). The following states have continuing education requirements as of June, 2015:

Alabama	Nevada
Alaska	New Hampshire
Arkansas	New Jersey
California	New Mexico
Delaware	New York
District of Columbia	North Carolina
Florida	North Dakota
Georgia	Ohio
Idaho	Oregon
Illinois	Rhode Island
Iowa	Pennsylvania
Kansas	South Carolina
Kentucky	Texas
Louisiana	Utah
Massachusetts	Washington
Michigan	West Virginia
Minnesota	Wyoming
Nebraska	West Virginia

Figure 7-1. States with Continuing Education Requirements.

Professional Practice Model

Magnet organizations, as well as those on a Magnet journey, are required to develop a Professional Practice Model (PPM), which nurses then utilize to drive their decisions about patient care and outcomes. Many organizations struggle to understand what is meant by a PPM and what the ANCC's requirements are.

A review of the literature uncovers the following definitions for the word *model*:

- A pattern of already existing events that can be learned and therefore repeated. A model represents procedures and sequences. (Hersey & Blanchard, 1996)

- A model is a schematic description . . . A model makes sense of a complex reality. (Wolf & Greenhouse, 2007)

- An overarching conceptual framework for nurses, nursing care, and interdisciplinary patient care. It is a schematic description of a system, theory, or phenomenon that depicts how nurses practice, collaborate, communicate, and develop professionally to provide the highest quality of care. (ANCC, 2008, p. 28)

Your PPM can have additional areas of focus as deemed appropriate by your organization, as long as the basic elements of clinical practice, communication, collaboration, and professional development are incorporated into your model. Organizations build their PPMs on a variety of theoretical frameworks, the most common being Relationship-Based Care (Creative Health Care Management, www.chcm.com) and the Synergy Model (American Association of Critical-Care Nurses, www.aacn.com). If you choose one of these frameworks, you need to amplify it to ensure that your PPM addresses how the nurses in your organization develop professionally. The PPM examples seen in Figures 7-2, 7-3, and 7-4 were each developed by the staffs at their respective organizations through a facilitative process.

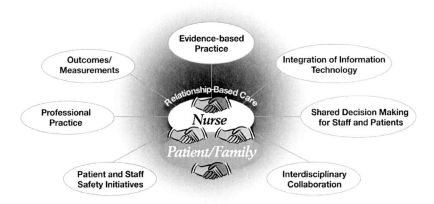

Professional Nursing Practice Model

Figure 7-2. York Hospital PPM (© York Hospital Nursing, York, Pennsylvania. Used with permission).

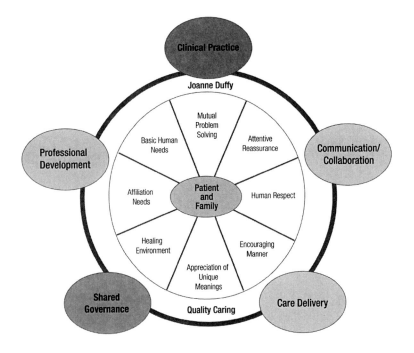

Lowell General Hospital Professional Practice Model 2009

Figure 7-3. Lowell General Hospital PPM (© Lowell General Hospital, Lowell, Massachusetts. Used with permission).

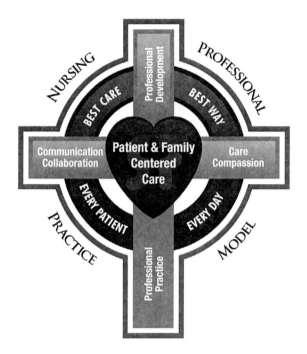

Figure 7-4. St. Francis Hospital PPM (© St Francis Hospital, Columbus, GA. Used with permission).

The creation of the schematic depiction is only the beginning. Since the PPM is only a "picture," staff will need reference or foundation documents to help them understand what drives the various elements of their model. The element of clinical practice includes their state Nurse Practice Act, their RN licensure, the ANA Code of Ethics, evidence-based practice, specialty standards of care and guidelines, and care delivery system(s). Without this foundation document, staff may not understand that they use the elements of the PPM every day and with every patient.

In the remaining chapters, we will look more closely at several of the remaining tenets of professional practice. These include the control of nursing practice and the practice environment, peer review and feedback, evidence-based practice, and rewards and recognition.

EIGHT

EMPOWERING PROFESSIONALS: CONTROL OF NURSING PRACTICE AND THE PRACTICE ENVIRONMENT

For many years, clinical nurses have been told how to do their work, when to do it, and what equipment to use to accomplish their work. More often than not, the people doing the telling were far removed from the actual point of care. Materials Management decides which IV pumps to purchase. Nursing Leadership creates the policy and procedure for the IV pump. Staff Development completes the IV pump education—and then the staff rebel.

In the 1970s and 1980s, management gurus identified that "companies demonstrating excellence were replacing traditional bureaucratic structures with governance structures that emphasized employee participation and involvement" (Schein, 1999). The age of the employee voice had finally arrived. The word *empowerment* was added to the dictionary and defined as "to give the means, ability, or opportunity to do" (YourDictionary, 2015).

The early days of nurse empowerment were rocky, to say the least. Contributing factors included the social and cultural view of women in the workforce, the dominant role of physicians in hospitals, and confusion over what empowerment was. Many misinterpreted it to mean 100% control or domination, as opposed to having the ability to act (Manojlovich, 2007).

Manojlovich describes three types of power that nurses must have to ensure maximum input into their work environment: control over the content of practice, control over the context of practice, and control over competence. Noted nurse researcher Marlene Kramer describes autonomy as the "freedom to act on what one knows,"— essentially as control over the content of nursing practice. "Staff nurses describe control over nursing practice (C/NP) as a professional nursing function made up of a variety of activities and outcomes. Greater acclaim, status, and prestige for nursing in the organization are viewed as a result, not a precursor, of C/NP" (Kramer, 2003).

In 1985, Prescott and Dennis stated that "nurses should be more meaningfully involved in the running of hospitals" (Prescott & Dennis, quoted in Swihart, 2006). Prior to the 1980s, including a nurse on the executive management team was unheard of. Now it is not unusual to have a CEO or COO who is a nurse. A requirement of

Magnet-designated organizations is that the chief nursing officer (CNO) must sit on the highest-level decision-making body and must have responsibility for all nursing practice. While not a Magnet requirement, a voting voice in these decision-making bodies speaks volumes about nursing's control of the practice environment, as well as how nursing is viewed by the organization's culture.

Shared Governance

One of nursing's shared governance pioneers, Tim Porter-O'Grady, states that only 10% of unit-level decisions should be made by management (Porter-O'Grady, quoted in Swihart, 2006). Yet even today, many organizations oppose this approach. Shared governance, or shared decision making, is based on four general principles:

- Partnership
- Equity
- Accountability
- Ownership

Porter-O'Grady (2003) defines shared governance as "a structural model through which nurses can express and manage their practice with a higher level of professional autonomy." In the early days of shared governance many leaders misinterpreted it to mean self-governance. Some managers abdicated their responsibilities to staff with little support to ensure success, while other managers confused participatory management with shared decision making.

In addition, staff confused shared governance with self-governance or the ability to make 100% of the decisions.

The differences between self-governance, participatory management, and shared governance can be seen in Figure 8-1.

Parameter	Self-Governance	Participatory Management	Shared Governance
Goals	Staff determine goals without input from leaders.	Leaders request input from staff; use of input is optional.	Staff are give the responsibility, authority and accountability for decisions.
Use of input	Can foster a "we/they" mindset.	Leader is not required to use staff input.	Leadership and staff activities are interdependent.
How decisions are made	All decisions made by work team with no external input or guidance.	Final decision lies with leadership, who may accept or reject staff input.	Leaders clearly articulate the guidelines for the decision (e.g., We have $10,000 to spend on __).
Presence of leader	Absent leader	Hierarchical leader	Servant leader
Where decisions are made		Centralized decision making	Decentralized decision making

Figure 8-1. Comparison of Management Styles.

In a decentralized, shared decision-making culture, decisions are made at the level of action by the people in the best position to judge their outcomes. The outcomes of shared decision making include:

- Promotion of autonomy.
- Enhancement of critical thinking skills.
- Creation of a learning environment.

In *Shared Governance: A Practical Approach to Reshaping Professional Nursing Practice* (2006), Diane Swihart defines four elements that are required for successful implementation of shared governance:

1. A committed nurse executive must be invested in process empowerment and must be willing to undertake the efforts necessary to implement shared governance.

2. A strong management team must be in place and committed to one another, to nursing, to the organization, and to the implementation process.

3. Shared governance cannot be implemented if the employees do not have a basic understanding of it and if they cannot build on that understanding with a working knowledge of what is to be accomplished. There must be a clear destination.

4. The plan and timeline for implementation are critical for charting progress points (Swihart, 2006).

Responsibility, Authority, and Accountability (RAA)

In addition to the preceding points, a complete understanding of responsibility, authority, and accountability (RAA) is required before a decentralized structure can succeed. Many times, staff willingly take on the decision-making authority, but they often balk at taking the responsibility and, even more, the accountability of the shared decision-making process. It is leadership's role to ensure that staff understand that shared decision making requires all three components—the complete package of RAA.

Responsibility ("Respond with Ability")

- Clear and specific allocation of duties in order to achieve desired results.
- Responsibility is visibly given and accepted.
- Personal ownership and aligned action are evident.

Authority

- The right to act and make decisions.
- Restricted to areas where responsibility is given and accepted.
- Consists of four levels (see Figure 8-2).

Accountability ("Account for Ability"):

- Inherent in the role.
- Reflecting on actions and decisions.
- Evaluating effectiveness. (Koloroutis, 2004)

Levels of Authority	
Level 1	*Data/Information/Idea Gathering* Authority to collect information/data and provide to another to make the final decision and determine what action will be taken.
Level 2	*Data/Information/Idea Gathering + Recommendations* Authority to collect information, weigh the options and recommend actions to be taken to another who will make final decision.
Level 3	*Data/Information/Idea Gathering + Recommendations (Pause to communicate, clarify or negotiate) + Take Action* Authority to apply critical thinking, weigh the options, recommend actions, negotiate the final decision. Includes pausing and collaborating with others before taking action.
Level 4	*Act + Inform others after taking action* Authority to assess, decide, and act. May follow up and inform another of the actions taken as required by the situation.

Figure 8-2. Four Levels of Authority (Manthey, 1994).

For a simple example of the Four Levels of Authority, let's consider the following scenario. You are new to a town and want to have lunch.

- **Level 1**: Others would gather information (names, menus, prices, and locations of restaurants) and give these to you.

- **Level 2**: Others would gather information (names, menus, prices, and locations of restaurants), give these to you, and recommend the best place to eat.

- **Level 3**: Others would gather information (names, menus, prices, and locations of restaurants), give these to you, and recommend the best place to eat. You then have an opportunity to ask questions and gather additional recommendations. After this pause, you decide where you want to have lunch.

- **Level 4**: Someone informs you of the lunch reservation they made for you.

Council Structures

To move forward in implementing decentralized decision making and shared governance, structures and processes must be put in place. Although different shared governance models exist (congressional, council, and administrative), most organizations choose a council structure in which there is representation from all areas in which nurses practice. In larger organizations, the resulting council size could create a barrier to productivity. For this reason, larger organizations may choose to have representatives from service delivery areas. For example, a member from the Maternal-Child service delivery area might be the voice for Labor and Delivery, Post-partum, Newborn Nursery, Special Care Nursery, Neonatal ICU, and Pediatrics. Many organizations go one step further by creating multidisciplinary councils from the beginning or developing plans to incorporate other disciplines in the future. Research/EBP councils are often early adopters of this interprofessional approach.

Council structure should begin with a general oversight council, often called the Results Council, Coordinating Council, Steering Council, or Leadership Council. Regardless of the name, this is the group that guides the decentralized decision making process throughout the organization. Membership consists of leaders and staff. After the development of the oversight council, additional councils are developed. The number and focus of these councils are based on organizational structure and need; at a minimum, councils responsible for practice, quality, research/EBP, and professional development are strongly recommended. Regardless of the number of councils, there should be a structure in place to ensure communication among all the councils. This mitigates the silo mentality that could develop without this communication structure.

Examples of councils that report to or are part of the coordinating council are shown in Figure 8-3 and could include:

- Practice Council.
- Performance Improvement or Quality Council.
- Research/Evidence-based Practice Council.
- Professional Development Council.
- Results Council.
- Leadership Council.
- Steering Council.

Figure 8-2. Example of Council Structure.

Building Council Competence

"A necessary precursor for both autonomy and empowerment is competence. Nurses must own their ongoing development to ensure that they are viewed as having expertise as opposed to just experience" (Manojlovich, 2007; Kramer, 2003). Years of experience must not be confused with expertise. We have all known nurses who have several years of experience but who lack the clinical expertise to affect patient outcomes. For this reason, all council members should receive education about the council structure and processes so that they can learn the skills listed in Figure 8-4.

- Negotiation
- Meeting management
- Decision making via consensus
- Conflict resolution
- Assertive communication
- Effective discussion
- Facilitation
- Team building
- Change management

Figure 8-4. Council Member Education Topics.

Ongoing education is also needed as council leadership changes and new members join. Wise organizations conduct annual shared governance education to enhance members' skills and ability.

It is through education that council members as well as leaders will develop clarity of purpose, competence, and confidence to accomplish their goals through collaboration (which in turn leads to true commitment), as well as the ability to effect change for improved outcomes (see Figure 8-5).

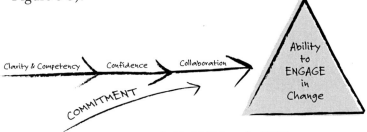

Figure 8-5. The 5 Cs Model (Koloroutis, 2004).

Unit-level Councils

The final level of councils resides in the units. Unit Practice Councils (UPCs) or Unit-Based Councils (UBCs) are made up of unit-specific representatives whose role is to identify and address unit-specific structures, processes, outcomes, issues, and concerns. Many units begin their UPCs with the representatives who sit on the larger councils. They then augment the UPC through the addition of other members. Many times these additional members are identified by asking staff, "Who would you trust to make decisions for you?" Some organizations utilize a nomination and election process, while others use an application process.

The members of the UPC are charged with the critical responsibility to communicate and garner feedback from an assigned cadre of fellow staff members. They are making decisions for the greater good of their unit, and a formal communication structure ensures input from all members of the unit.

The Manager's Purely Facilitative Role

When organizations implement a decentralized, shared decision-making structure, they often overlook the support that managers need in order to facilitate the process. Giving up what has been major control of their units can be threatening or frightening to some managers. Education, support, and coaching about the benefits, outcomes, and skills needed for successful implementation of shared decision making must be given special attention. Keep in mind that shared governance and shared decision making won't work if the manager won't let it, and it is, of course, hard to let something happen if you do not understand it.

Many organizations have reported early shared decision making success through the use of a facilitator, whose primary role is to help the council move forward by paying attention to group process. If you choose to go in that direction, remember that true facilitators have no vested interest in the end result or the decisions made. Facilitators do not own the process or group; they are not group leaders. Facilitators also benefit from education so that they can be skilled in group process and ensure that they facilitate and not own the group.

The Importance of Periodic Assessments

Regardless of the structure of your councils, attention should be paid to a periodic, comprehensive assessment of their functionality and effectiveness. This assessment should include a review of:

- What's working well?
- What needs improvement?
- What outcomes have been realized?
- What best practices in structures and processes are being operationalized?
- What structural improvements can be made (e.g., meeting times, length, membership, etc.)?

It is not unusual to hear stories of organizations that have been engaged in shared governance for many years, taking time periodically to rebuild or restructure their systems and processes and seeing enhanced outcomes as a result.

Attention to education for participants and managers, periodic effectiveness review, and revisions to structures and processes will lead to a stronger, more vibrant shared decision-making culture.

There is nothing more difficult to take in hand, more perilous to conduct, or more uncertain in its success, than to take the lead in the introduction of a new order of things.
—NICCOLÒ MACHIAVELLI, *THE PRINCE* (1532)

NINE

So How Am I Doing?
Creating Peer Review/Feedback
Systems That Work

Some nurses, especially those who work "off shifts" and weekends only, are frustrated after their annual appraisals. They may comment, "How can my manager really evaluate me since we never work together?" Nurse managers also struggle with the responsibility of evaluating staff with whom they have little interaction. Many managers do make an effort to work beside each of their staff members at least once during the year. This gives them a view of the individual nurse's work; however, this practice is limited. As more and more organizations foster nursing professional practice, they are turning to peer review and feedback systems that foster professional development and accountability.

What is Peer Review?

According to the American Nurses Association (ANA), "peer review is an organized effort whereby practicing professionals review the quality and appropriateness of services ordered or performed by their professional peers. Peer review in nursing is the process by which practicing RNs systematically assess, monitor, and make judgments about the quality of nursing care provided by peers as measured against professional standards of practice" (ANA, 1978b).

Let's consider an alternative definition of peer review: an active supportive practice to professionally acknowledge and enhance a colleague's performance. The key words in this definition are *active*, *supportive*, *enhance*, and *performance*. These are the attributes that must be present in every peer review experience to ensure that it is viewed as an opportunity for development instead of a punitive experience.

Most intellectual disciplines include peer review as an integral component of their practice. Nursing has identified peer review as a tenet of professional practice. According to research, 95% of staff and 100% of nurse managers preferred a process of peer review as opposed to leadership only review (Lower, 2007). Peer review:

- Facilitates the development of skills for effective feedback.
- Enhances the reviewee's professional practice, professional development, and education.

- Fosters collegial conversations about patient care.

Peer Review in the Sources of Evidence

Of the Sources of Evidence Within the Magnet Model, Exemplary Professional Practice (EP) specifically addresses peer review:

> **EP 15:** Nurses at all levels engage in periodic formal performance reviews that include a self-appraisal and peer feedback process for assurance of competence and continuous professional development (ANCC, 2013, p. 47).

The Joint Commission also advocates for the development of peer review systems to further support nursing professional practice.

The development of a peer review and feedback system needs careful consideration and staff involvement. As you contemplate the development of your peer review and feedback system, you should evaluate what, if any, peer review your organization is already conducting. You will be quite surprised! Informal *and* formal peer review is already happening in your organization. From an informal perspective, nurses know who they want, or don't want, to follow when starting their shift. They know who they would go to for assistance. They know who they would want to care for themselves or a family member, and who they would avoid. They know the strengths and opportunities for improvement of every nurse they work with.

Formal peer reviews include precepted orientations, chart audits by staff nurses, incident report investigations conducted by nurse risk managers, skills reviews and demonstrations, mock drills, competency assessment programs, national certification, institution-specific certifications such as for chemotherapy administration, and skills certification programs such as BLS, ACLS, and PALS taught by nurses. See Figure 9-1.

SAMPLE PEER REVIEW ACTIVITIES

Chart audit

Skills lab redemonstration

BLS certification

ACLS certification

Precepted orientation

Clinical ladder programs

State licensure

Incident report investigations

National certification

Institutional certification

Competency assessment programs

Figure 9-1. Examples of Peer Review Activities (Guanci, 2007).

Although these examples are indeed considered peer review for a journey to Magnet designation, the ANCC is looking for a more formal structure and process. The ideal peer review and feedback system contains both formal and informal review. Peer review and feedback should be a continuous, developmental process, not just an annual evaluation. It includes three distinct foci: routine peer feedback, peer competence assessment/validation, and case-based or incident-based peer review. The ultimate peer review is real-time, one-on-one feedback. To achieve this, we must become competent in having difficult conversations, especially since most of us grew up being taught, "If you cannot say something nice, don't say anything at all." It is this real-time, informal communication that will support the ultimate goals of peer review: ongoing professional development, validation of competence, and continuous strengthening of the organization's professional practice environment.

The Role of Nursing Councils in Developing Peer Review

Many organizations utilize one of their nursing councils to spearhead development of the peer review system. The council is charged with developing the structure, the process guidelines, and the tool that will be used. Questions the council will need to answer include:

- What type of case-based/incident-based peer review will we have?

- What type of personal and professional growth peer feedback will we have?

- How will the review process support our professional practice model?

- How many reviewers will there be?
- Who will select the reviewers?
- How often will formal reviews be conducted?
- How will informal peer feedback be tracked?
- How unit-specific will the process be?
- What dimensions of practice will be reviewed?
- What format will the tool utilize (rating scale, open-ended questions, narrative, or a combination)?
- Will the tool mirror the general employee evaluation?
- How will the reviewee receive the information?
- Will peer reviewers be anonymous or identified?

Whatever structure and process you develop, you need guidelines to ensure safety for:

- The individual receiving feedback.
- The individual giving feedback.
- The manager interpreting the feedback.

Figure 9-2 outlines elements of successful peer review and feedback.

The individual being reviewed is responsible for his/her professional growth—not the reviewer.

Peer review is confidential.

Peer review and feedback are collaborative activities.

Peer review and feedback are both formal and informal.

Peer review and feedback identify opportunities for professional growth.

Peer review and feedback enhance personal professional growth for all parties involved.

Peer review and feedback are supportive.

Peer review and feedback are ongoing.

Peer review and feedback are safe for all parties involved.

The peer review and feedback systems must fit your organizational culture.

Figure 9-2. Elements of Effective Peer Review and Feedback (Guanci, 2007).

Staff Education on the Peer Review Process

Regardless of what peer review and feedback processes your organization designs and implements, consideration must be given to what education staff will receive in order to ensure a successful process. Many nurses will admit that they feel unprepared to give developmental feedback to colleagues. They will gladly tell colleagues all the wonderful things they do, but when it comes to advising colleagues about their areas for growth, many nurses clam up. The need for these developmental conversations mandates that we educate and coach staff to their fullest potential. Education must include a didactic presentation that reviews components of effective feedback, as well as the opportunity to role-play and receive coaching.

When implementing your peer review and feedback processes, it is recommended that you start slowly and set up systems that ensure early successes and positive experiences. Although peer review can be intimidating initially, it fosters a professional practice environment in which colleagues care for each other's professional development and coach each other toward their developmental goals. Figure 9-3 offers an example of peer feedback built on the components of one organization's professional practice model. Figure 9-4 shows the professional practice model: practice, communication, collaboration, and professional development.

STAMFORD HOSPITAL | The Regional Center for Health

Individualized Peer Feedback Guidelines/ Examples

Describe situations in which the RN has demonstrated actions in each of the components of the Stamford Hospital Nursing Professional Practice Model.

I. With patient centered care, the nurse demonstrates the ability to offer whatever comfort the clinical situation requires or allows to support the patient and or family. Describe a situation where you observed the nurse exhibiting these skills.

II. In the collaboration domain, the nurse demonstrates the ability to make proficient decisions based on prior experiences and collaborates with patients/ families and interdisciplinary team members. Describe a situation where you observed the nurse exhibiting these skills.

III. In the practice domain, the nurse demonstrates expert clinical practice and foresight in the care of the culturally diverse patient. Describe a situation where you observed the nurse exhibiting these skills.

IV. In the communication domain, the nurse demonstrates the ability to communicate effectively with the patient/family and interdisciplinary team members. Describe a situation where you observed the nurse exhibiting these skills.

V. Identify an area (or areas) you believe this nurse could focus on for professional development over the course of the next year.

July 2014 Professional Development Council

Page 1

Figure 9-3. Stamford Hospital Peer Feedback Form (Copyright 2014, Stamford Hospital, Stamford, CT. Used with permission).

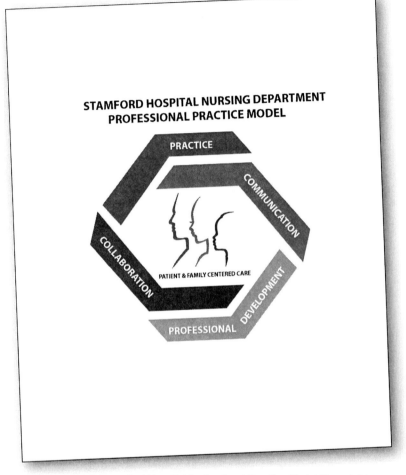

Figure 9-4. Stamford Hospital Professional Practice Model (Copyright Stamford Hospital, Stamford, CT. Used with permission).

TEN

GETTING STARTED IN EVIDENCE-BASED PRACTICE AND NURSING RESEARCH

Evidence-based practice (EBP) in nursing is the "process by which nurses make clinical decisions using the best available research evidence" (University of Minnesota School of Nursing, 2000). However, mention the words *evidence-based practice* or *nursing research* to many nurses, and you may be met with uncertainty. Only about 15% of health care providers use EBP when making clinical decisions (Cipriano, 2007). The move to the electronic health record and, in particular, to computerized physician order entry is fostering the use of order sets that are built on and routinely updated with the latest evidence.

EBP is not new to nursing. In the 1850s, Florence Nightingale examined factors affecting the morbidity and mortality of soldiers during the Crimean War. She kept extensive logs of patients' responses to care. Her findings identified the need for sanitary conditions when caring for the sick and injured. Nightingale disseminated her findings and implemented practice changes that led to reductions in mortality. The summary of her research, *Notes on Nursing*, was published in 1860.

Why do Nursing Research?

And for that matter, why use evidence-based practice? Why not just use medical research? Incorporating nursing research and evidence-based practice into clinical decisions demonstrates our professional accountability to our patients. The use of nursing research and evidence to inform practice reinforces the identity of nursing as an intellectual discipline and a profession. In addition, it fortifies the tenet that nurses, not physicians or others involved in the delivery of health care, are responsible for nursing practice. Lastly, not using EBP is tantamount to negligence. The nursing practice of yesterday—"This is the way we do it" and "This is the way we have always done it"—has been replaced by "This is the way it is done, because . . . ."

A 2007 review of literature by Karkos and Peters identified multiple barriers to the implementation and use of evidence-based care (see Figure 10-1). The lack of time to read EBP literature was ranked the number one barrier. In addition to time to read the literature, nurses need dedicated time, free from patient care responsibilities, to develop and implement strategies to create a culture of inquiry and critical thinking. Support from nursing leadership, and the organization in general, is needed in the form of time, finances, and resources to sustain a culture of inquiry. Today many organizations are implementing structures and processes and making available the resources needed to support EBP.

Top 10 Nursing Barriers to the Use of Evidence-Based Care

1. Lack of time to read.

2. Lack of authority to make changes.

3. Lack of time to implement new ideas.

4. Unawareness of research.

5. Lack of physician support for implementation.

6. Relevant literature not together in one place.

7. Inability to understand statistical analyses.

8. Overwhelming amount of information.

9. Belief that results are not pertinent to current work setting.

10. Does not feel capable of evaluating the quality of research.

Figure 10-1. Top Ten Nursing Barriers to the Use of Evidence-Based Care (Adapted from "Magnet Community Hospital: Fewer Barriers to Nursing Research Utilization," by B. Karkos and K. Peters, 2007, *Journal of Nursing Administration, 36*(7–8), pp. 377–382. Adapted with permission).

Nurses' knowledge deficit about EBP is often grounded in insufficient general knowledge about the research process, including knowing the difference between qualitative and quantitative research, understanding the various EBP models, translating research into clinical practice, and being aware of available resources to support the use of best practice guidelines.

Integrating EBP into Daily Practice

Organizations wishing to build a framework for a culture of clinical inquiry must develop a strategic plan for implementation. Essential to the plan is the development of a learning community via education, as well as ongoing coaching and mentoring. Even though the goal of the plan would be to launch EBP and nursing research, communication to the staff may very well determine the plan's success or failure. To tell staff that they *will* be using EBP may be perceived as negative. Instead, why not introduce the topic in the form of a study group? This is a safe invitation to those who, while intrigued, may not be willing to admit that their knowledge of EBP is limited. The study group can cover topics such as understanding the research process, ethical aspects related to research, interpretation of reports, determination of study validity and data collection methods, and a comparison of EBP models.

The implementation of EBP into daily practice requires that staff members have easy access to journals, references, and best practice guidelines. Several comprehensive nurse-specific resources are on the market today.

Many of these products are available through an institutional license that enables nurses to access them via their organization's intranet. Resources for EBP and best practice guidelines include:

- Registered Nurses' Association of Ontario (RNAO): http://www.rnao.ca

- Joanna Briggs Institute: http://www.joannabriggs.org

- University Health Network of Canada: http://www.uhn.ca

- National Guideline Clearinghouse: http://www.guideline.gov

- Specialty organization websites (e.g., AACN Practice Alerts): http://www.aacn.org

- ACE Star Model of Knowledge Transformation (Stevens): http://www.acestar.uthscsa.edu/acestar-model.asp

- Iowa Model of EBP to Promote Quality of Care: http://www.uihealthcare.org/otherservices.aspx?id=1617

- Evidence Based Nursing journal: http://ebn.bmj.com

- University of York Health Sciences Research Department http://www.york.ac.uk/healthsciences/research/

- Nursing and Allied Health Resources Section: http://nahrs.mlanet.org/
- National Network of Libraries of Medicine (NN/LM): http://www.nlm.nih.gov/
- NAHRS Task Force on Mapping the Literature of Nursing: http://nahrs.mlanet.org/home/activities/mapnur

EBP is challenging many of the procedures we used to do (the sacred cows of nursing), including:

- Use of milk, Maalox, and heat lamps for open decubiti.
- Rotating tourniquets for pulmonary edema.
- Enemas for all women in labor.
- Ice caps for patients receiving chemotherapy.
- Suctioning intubated patients every 2 hours with instilled saline.

Examples of nursing practice changes reported through professional organizations and journals include:

- Elevating the head of the bed for intubated patients to decrease the incidence of ventilator-associated pneumonia (American Association of Critical-Care Nurses, 2008).
- Use of 0.5% chlorhexidine on central line dressing to reduce the incidence of catheter-related sepsis (Centers for Disease and Prevention [CDC], 2012). Completion of

medication reconciliation (Joint Commission, 2007).

- Use of care bundles to decrease catheter-associated urinary tract infections (CDC, 2015)

- Use of 6-hour sepsis bundle (Surviving Sepsis Campaign, 2015).

In addition to easy access to EBP resources, a model for EBP should be chosen to ensure consistent and thorough evaluation of available research. EBP models walk staff through the determination of whether or not the evidence is sufficient and applicable to their type of organization, as well as the potential limitations of the evidence. A standardized approach will foster familiarity and a level of comfort with EBP among staff nurses. Well-known models include:

- The Iowa Model of EBP to Promote Quality of Care.

- ACE Star Model of Knowledge Transformation (Stevens, 2012).

- The Stetler Model of Research Utilization.

- The Ottawa Model of Research Use.

- Evidence-Based Multidisciplinary Practice Model.

- A Model for Change to Evidence-Based Practice.

- The Center for Advanced Nursing Practice model.

Regardless of the model chosen, there are six major steps in translating literature into practice:

1. Ask the question.

2. Search the literature.

3. Critically analyze the evidence.

4. Identify the evidence you will apply.

5. Apply the evidence.

6. Measure and evaluate your evidence application.

Taking on EBP and Nursing Research

We must be clear that EBP and nursing research are not the same thing. If after reviewing the literature you find a lack of evidence, this indicates that the topic would benefit from a research study. If your organization does not have a designated nurse researcher, there are several strategies to facilitate success. First, find a nursing research mentor. This could be a professor from a local college of nursing or a professional nurse researcher. If you are a nurse, perhaps the professor who taught *you* about nursing research/EBP would be honored to continue to foster clinical inquiry. To bring a nursing research study into your organization, partner with a school of nursing. After all, the school's tenured faculty are required to publish research. Let them know that your organization is willing to support their efforts to recruit subjects, with the understanding that they will engage one or more of your nurses as a coinvestigator of the study, receive approval from your institutional review board (IRB), and disseminate the study results throughout your organization. One example is the community hospital that partnered with renowned nurse researcher Marlene Kramer and facilitated research interviews with staff nurses about clinical autonomy (Kramer, 2003).

When your organization is ready to conduct independent research, consider replicating a previous study. This will ease the burden of developing the research problem, question, and/or hypothesis. One study that many organizations have chosen to replicate is the effect of hourly rounding on the use of patient call lights (Meade, Bursell, & Ketelsen, 2006). Staff nurses see the value of this type of research because it relates to their daily work.

Another study to replicate that introduces research concepts and principles while having fun is The Great American Cookie Experiment. First conducted in the early 1970s, it has been replicated numerous times throughout the nursing world. The study introduces participants to the principles of quantitative and qualitative research as it explores participant preferences related to a variety of types of chocolate chip cookies.

Other initial steps include fulfilling the requirement that all staff involved in conducting research complete education in the protection of human subjects as well as obtaining the approval of the research study by the organization's IRB. Be sure the IRB has a formal registered nurse member and documents his or her vote on all nursing research studies. The IRB may be an internal or outsourced board whose purpose is:

> To assure, both in advance and by periodic review, that appropriate steps are taken to protect the rights and welfare of humans participating as subjects in a research study. To accomplish this purpose, IRBs review research protocols and related materials (e.g., informed consent documents and investigator brochures) to ensure protection of the rights and welfare of human subjects of research. The chief objectives of every IRB protocol review are to assess the ethics of the research and its methods, to promote fully informed and voluntary participation by prospective subjects who are themselves capable of making such choices (or, if that is not possible, informed permission given by a suitable proxy) and to maximize the safety of subjects once they are enrolled in the project (Institutional Review Board, n.d.).

The conducting of nursing research and its translation into evidence-based practice continues to grow. The Magnet Recognition Program® is in part responsible for this advance, since nursing research and the use of EBP are significant requirements. Regardless of the reason, many organizations who have moved forward with nursing research and EBP have found that their staff was "just waiting to be asked." Be sure to celebrate your successes as you bring EBP to the bedside!

ELEVEN

KEEPING EXCELLENT NURSES: REWARD AND RECOGNITION PROGRAMS

Much has been written about the human need for recognition. According to Terry Bacon, author of *What People Want: A Manager's Guide to Building Relationships That Work*, "Recognition for a job well done is critical" (Bacon, 2006, p. xvii). Even though it is the responsibility of leaders to coach employees to their maximum performance, they often fail to use the simplest technique of all. Simply recognizing the behavior they want, when they see it, is highly effective. Rewards and recognitions programs can offer the opportunity for customized recognition.

Trends Affecting Leaders

There is no doubt about it, the work environment of today differs from that of 20, 10, 5, and even 2 years ago. The trends that affect leaders today are many and complex. These trends can be divided into two categories: those that are business-driven and those that are employee-driven.

Business-Driven Trends

The shortage of nurses and other health care workers is alive and well. According to the Bureau of Labor Statistics' Employment Projections 2012–2022, (Bureau of Labor Statistics, 2013), registered nursing is among the top occupations in terms of job growth through 2022. The RN workforce is expected to grow from 2.71 million in 2012 to 3.24 million in 2022, an increase of 526,800 or 19%. The Bureau also projects the need for 525,000 replacement nurses, bringing the total number of job openings for nurses due to growth and replacements to 1.05 million by 2022.

Recruitment offers on the variety of Internet sites available for job seekers are full of enticing sign-on benefit options, including four- and five-figure sign-on bonuses, paid relocation expenses, free laptop computers, six-figure annual salaries, and school loan forgiveness programs. One recruitment ad even offered one year of paid biweekly house cleaning service—proof that organizations are thinking outside the box when it comes to recruitment efforts. It's all well and good to get employees on board;

however, organizations recognized for excellence are going beyond recruitment. They realize that retention is actually a higher priority than recruitment.

The Families and Work Institute reports that the turnover and replacement cost of one nonmanagerial employee is approximately $88,000. Replacement costs for a manager can be 150% of his or her annual salary (Krsek, 2011). This means that organizations with high turnover rates will spend millions of dollars replacing employees. Therefore it would behoove your organization to focus on retention to help control these costs.

Another business-driven trend is that technology in health care is moving closer to the bedside and the nursing care delivery team. Computerized nursing documentation, electronic medication administration records, and computerized physician order entry systems are leading to decreased "live" communication. The downside of the increased use of technology is that it often leads to a low-touch environment in systems where consumers demand high-touch. Many believe that increased use of technology at the bedside is to blame for the erosion of workforce communication skills and processes.

The final business-driven trend affecting recruitment and retention is time. Manufacturing has always known that the faster a product is produced, the more revenue is earned. Time equals money. This is true in health care, too. Improvements in financial metrics, such as shorter operating room turnaround times, are common goals for inpatient care areas. Patient throughput teams have sprung up across the country as organizations struggle to address processes that will facilitate a patient's progress into and out of the health care system.

Employee-Driven Trends

What do the increase in autonomous practice, shared governance, and professional practice environments have in common? They all share a need for greater employee initiative. Knowing what increases intrinsic motivation is a core competency for leaders today, yet little is done to increase this motivation until a problem is identified.

When asked to complete a ten-item ranking of what is important to their employees, leaders ranked "good wages" as number one and "feeling in on things" as number ten (Nelson, 1999). However, *employees* of that same organization ranked "full appreciation for work done" as number one and "feeling in on things" as number two; they ranked "good wages" number five (see Figure 11-1).

	LEADERS	EMPLOYEES
Full appreciation for work done	8	1
Feeling IN on things	10	2
Sympathetic help with personal problems	9	3
Job security	2	4
Good wages	1	5
Interesting work	5	6
Promotion/growth opportunities	3	7
Personal loyalty to workers	6	8
Good working conditions	4	9
Tactful disciplining	7	10

Figure 11-1. Workplace Issue Rank Ordering (Reprinted from Nelson, 1999. Copyright R. Nelson. Reprinted with permission).

Although originally conducted in 1994, this survey has been repeated several times in a wide variety of organization types and businesses since then with similar results.

Employees have spoken loudly and clearly: They want—no, they *demand*—recognition. In his 1999 article, "The Ten Ironies of Motivation," Bob Nelson identifies the challenges that accompany motivation and recognition (Figure 11-2). These ironies remain virtually unchanged to this day.

Ten Ironies of Motivation

1) Most managers think money is the top motivator—it is not.

2) "You get what you reward" is common sense, but not common practice.

3) Things that are most motivating to employees tend to be easy to do and cost effective.

4) What motivates others is different from what motivates you.

5) Simple, fun, and creative rewards work best.

6) The greatest impact in using formal awards comes from their symbolic value.

7) Recognizing good performance will result in more of the behavior.

8) Managers do not focus on employee motivation until it is lost.

9) It takes less effort to sustain desired behavior than to initially create it.

10) The more you help employees develop marketable skills the more likely they are to stay with your organization.

Figure 11-2. Ten Ironies of Motivation (Reprinted from © Robert Nelson. Reprinted with permission).

In addition to full appreciation for work done, an ANA *SmartBrief* article stated that progress toward goal and recognition of that progress are prime motivators for nursing staff (ANA, 2010).

Reward and Recognition Programs

Before establishing any reward and recognition program, a leader must know what types of recognition work for *each* employee. Employees no longer want cookie-cutter rewards. They are looking for rewards that are meaningful to them. Rewards must be meaningful and authentic, not automatic (Biro, 2013). The wise leader will ask questions about the workplace. Ask your employees, "What are the things that keep you here?" "What frustrates you so much that you sometimes want to leave?" "What would you do if you were in my shoes?"

Another approach is a "Do More, Do Less, Continue to Do" questionnaire. Once a year, ask your employees: "What do you wish I would do more of?" "What do you wish I would do less of?" and "What do you want me to continue to do the same?" Remember: Before asking these questions, you must be committed to acting on the results. Asking questions, getting responses, and then ignoring those responses is a recipe for decreasing motivation.

In addition to informal assessment, routine formal satisfaction surveys should be considered. The ability to drill down to individual job types and work areas is valuable in this process and will facilitate customized action plans. As with the informal process, before finding the answers to these questions, your organization's leaders must be committed to acting on the data.

Rewards That Work

So how can leaders reward and recognize employees on a limited budget?

Keep in mind, employees reported that money was not the top motivator—full appreciation of work done *is*. With this in mind, leaders need to be able to engage their staff. They need to be direct, flexible, and personal. Keep rewards and recognition balanced. Offer choices. Involve employees in the development of a rewards program by implementing a culture of shared governance. Be timely with your rewards. Create traditions. Individualize your rewards, use different strokes for different folks.

A simple yet effective tool for individualizing rewards is the Favorites List (Figure 11-3). Have all employees fill this out and keep their copies on file. When the time comes to reward an employee, you have a reference of his or her likes. Imagine giving an employee a basket of goodies filled with milk chocolate, only to find out that the person dislikes milk chocolate and eats only dark chocolate. Now imagine the delight when the same basket of goodies is filled with dark chocolate! Not only have you given something you know your employee will like, you have sent the message that you took the time to personalize his or her recognition.

Your Favorites List

Just for the fun of it I would like to know the following very important facts about you:

1) Name:
2) Favorite color:
3) Favorite candy or snack:
4) Favorite author:
5) Favorite movie theater:
6) Favorite hobby:
7) Favorite pampering method:
8) Favorite lotions and potions:
9) Favorite restaurant:
10) Favorite place to shop:
11) Favorite non-alcoholic beverage:
12) Favorite charity:

Figure 11-3. Example of a Favorites List (Guanci, 2007).

Another low-cost or no-cost recognition tip is sending handwritten notes. Many leaders already do this, but the retention-savvy leader takes it one step further by sending the note to the employee's home. In addition to notes, research has shown that retention increased with the use of certain key phrases (Nelson, 1999). While we often say, "You're doing great," increasing your kudos phrases to, "You are doing quality work on . . ." and "You've made my day because of . . ." will go a long way (see Figure 11-4). Simply using the individual's name can also go a long way in increasing motivation: "Sue, I'm really impressed with . . . ."

---

10 Phrases that Increase Retention and Motivation

"You really made a difference by . . ."

"I'm impressed with . . ."

"You got my attention when you . . ."

"You're doing top quality work on . . ."

"You're right on the mark with..."

"One of the things I enjoy most about you is . . ."

"You can be proud of yourself for . . ."

"We couldn't have done it with your . . ."

"What an effective way to . . ."

"You've made my day because of . . ."

Figure 11-4. 10 Phrases that Increase Retention and Motivation (Adapted from *Success Secrets* (p. 38) by M. McCormick, 1990, Waukegan, Illinois. Adapted with permission).

Create theme awards such as the ABCD Award (Above and Beyond the Call of Duty Award). Consider creating a "pass-along" award. Remember Buzz Lightyear from *Toy Story?* (See Chapter 2.) He is known for saying, "To infinity and beyond!" Purchase a Buzz doll that circulates among the staff. Whoever receives the Buzz Award is responsible for identifying the next recipient who has gone "To infinity and beyond." Think of rewards that are visible. Use rewards that let everyone know that the individual wearing the reward has been recognized for something special—buttons, pins, or ribbons work well. Or create slogan awards (Figure 11-5).

Possible Slogan Awards

You Make a Difference

Pat on the Back

Top Banana

Thanks for the Memories

The Jugglers

The Big Kahuna

Helping Hand Behind the Scenes

ABCD (Above and Beyond the Call of Duty)

Figure 11-5. Possible Slogan Awards.

Consider also recognizing individuals outside your department. This can be easily accomplished by starting each staff meeting with the question, "Is there anyone in another department we should recognize?" Examples could include a handwritten thank-you note to the shuttle drivers who drive you to and from the employee parking lot with a smile and a pleasant demeanor. Perhaps an individual in another department just received national certification. Write him or her a kudos note. An example of this is the organization whose security and facilities employees shoveled out nurses' cars during the historic Boston winter of 2015. Just imagine how those individuals would feel when others celebrate their work!

For many leaders, offering sincere recognition does not come easily. It is a skill that must be nurtured and practiced. If your recognition skills need work, make a commitment to finding three opportunities each day to recognize individuals. Just be sure it is sincere recognition; employees know right away when it is not! Soon it will become second nature, and the sky is the limit. If you need further motivation to recognize employees, keep in mind the phrase, "People do not leave a job . . . they leave a leader." Don't be that leader! Remember, every leader is a CRO—Chief Retention Officer!

AFTERWORD:
The Journey Never Ends

At some point, someone in your organization will ask you, "When will we be finished creating our culture of nursing excellence?" The truth is: In excellent organizations, the journey doesn't end; the bar keeps rising. Excellent organizations do not settle for the status quo. They are constantly asking themselves: What else? What's next? How can we make this even better? How can we be innovative? How do we raise the bar?

Although this book has identified several essentials found in cultures of excellence, there are many more. You may have a practice in your organization that strengthens and supports your culture of excellence. I encourage you to look at what is working in your organization, celebrate it, and then ask yourself: Is there anything else we can do to strengthen this?

The journey to excellence is not easy or straight. There will be times of joy and celebration mixed with frustration and even backward slides. The challenge will be to keep your vision of a culture of excellence and continue working hard to achieve this vision. I remember a CNO of a Magnet organization, six months after designation, saying to a few of her directors, "I never realized how much work it would be once we reached our designation!" The directors just looked at her and each other and said, "We know!"

> *What you get by reaching your destination*
> *isn't as important as what you* **BECOME** *by reaching*
> *your destination.*
> —Anonymous

APPENDIX A

SUMMARY OF CULTURES OF EXCELLENCE AWARDS & DESIGNATIONS

American Association of Critical-Care Nurses (AACN) Beacon Award for Excellence® Evaluation Categories

1. **Leadership Structures and Systems:** Evaluates the leadership style of the unit as well as the support for the professional practice environment. This includes the use of shared decision-making processes and individual accountability. 150 points

2. **Appropriate Staffing and Staff Engagement:** Looks at staff satisfaction as well as what the unit is doing related to benefits, employee development, and quality of life. 100 points

3. **Effective Communication, Knowledge Management, and Best Practices:** Includes the types of communication used to ensure continuity and coordination of multidisciplinary care and professional development activities and support, as well as efforts to ensure a healthy work environment. 100 points

4. **Evidence-Based Practice and Processes:** Reviews the unit's use of evidence-based protocols in the development of nursing practice as well as staff access to evidence-based practice resources. In addition, use of best practices is also evaluated. 200 points

5. **Patient Outcomes:** The largest category, looks at the overall outcomes of the unit as well as those related to specific disease processes. An evaluation of the adequacy of staffing is also completed. 450 points

Baldrige Performance Excellence Program (BPEP) Award Components

1. **Leadership:** Looks at how the organization is led, its responsibilities to the public, and how the organization practices good citizenship. 120 points

2. **Strategy:** Evaluates how the organization develops and deploys strategic direction. 85 points

3. **Customer:** Assesses how the organization proactively searches for and establishes sustained relationships with customers. 85 points

4. **Measurement, Analysis, and Knowledge Management:** Assesses how the organization identifies, collects, disseminates, and improves data and knowledge resources. 90 points

5. **Workforce:** Reviews how the organization is maximizing the workforce's potential, as well as aligning it with the organization's mission, vision, philosophy, and strategic plan. 85 points

6. **Operations:** Examines how the organization develops, deploys, and improves process management. This category is about process as opposed to results, which is addressed next. 85 points

7. **Results:** Counts toward 45% of the total points, which states loudly and clearly that the BPEP is about results. Not only are the organization's face-value results reviewed, they are benchmarked against those of competitors and other similar organizations. 450 points

American Nurses Credentialing Center (ANCC) Magnet Model

1. **Transformational Leadership (TL):** Includes strategic planning, advocacy and influence, visibility, accessibility, and communication.

2. **Structural Empowerment (SE):** Includes professional engagement, commitment to professional development, teaching and role development, commitment to the community, and recognition of nursing.

3. **Exemplary Professional Practice (EP):** The most comprehensive of the components, looks at professional practice model; care delivery system; staffing, scheduling and budget processes; interdisciplinary care; accountability, competence and autonomy; ethics, privacy, security, and confidentiality; diversity and workplace advocacy; culture of safety; and quality care monitoring and improvement.

4. **New Knowledge, Innovations, and Improvements (NK):** Looks at research, evidence-based practice, and innovation.

5. **Empirical Outcomes (EO):** Addresses the "so what" or what is different as a result of the systems process and infrastructure that are in place (ANCC, 2014).

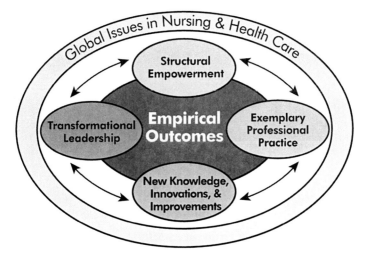

Figure A-1. The Magnet Model (© 2008 American Nurses Credentialing Center. All rights reserved. Reproduced with the permission of the American Nurses Credentialing Center).

American Nurses Credentialing Center (ANCC) Pathway to Excellence® Standards

- Nurses control the practice of nursing.
- The work environment is safe and healthy.
- Systems are in place that address patient care and practice.
- Orientation prepares new nurses.
- The CNO is qualified and participates in all levels of the facility.
- Professional development is provided and utilized.
- Competitive wages/salaries are in place.
- Nurses are recognized for achievements.
- A balanced lifestyle is encouraged.
- Collaborative interdisciplinary relationships are valued and supported.
- Nurse managers are competent and accountable.
- A quality program and evidence-based practices are utilized.

BPEP and Magnet Recognition® Crosswalk

BPEP Values/Concepts	Forces of Magnetism	Magnet Model Component
Visionary leadership	Quality of nursing leadership	Transformational leadership (TL)
Systems perspective	Organizational structure	Structural empowerment (SE)
Managing for innovation	Management style	Transformational leadership (TL)
Valuing staff, partners & customers Staff focus	Personnel policies and programs Interdisciplinary relationships	Structural empowerment (SE) Exemplary professional practice (EP)
Patient focused excellence	Professional models of care Quality of care	Exemplary professional practice (EP) New knowledge, innovations, and improvements (NK)
Management by fact	Quality improvement	New knowledge, innovations, and improvements (NK)
Focus on results & creating value	Consultation and resources	Exemplary professional practice (EP)
Agility	Autonomy	Exemplary professional practice (EP)
Social responsibility and community health	Community and the hospital	Structural empowerment (SE)
Organizational and personal learning	Nurses as teachers Professional development	Exemplary professional practice (EP) Structural empowerment (SE)
Focus on the future	Image of nurses	Structural empowerment (SE)

APPENDIX B

WEB-BASED MAGNET DOCUMENTS

The ANCC is paperless as of February 2016. All Magnet documents must be submitted via either a website or thumb/flash drive. When it comes to deciding which way to go—web-based or thumb/flash drive—consider several things. Take the following survey to help you determine what you are looking for in your electronic format and what is best for your organization.

- I want to access my document anytime, from any computer and any location.

- I want to be able to make my own document edits or have them done by my document partner.

- I want expert guidance, review, and feedback regarding my document contents to maximize our potential for success.

- I want a live, always-on website that eliminates the stress of a "launch" date.
- I want a solution that is independent of my already busy IT department.
- I want a solution that does not rely on our server to host a Magnet document website.
- I want a structure and process to help facilitate accountability to our document timeline.
- I want to have the option of submitting my document via a website or flash drive and not have to make an early decision on which electronic format to use.

If you agree with any of these statements, start researching web-based Magnet document services right away. I had the honor of helping Creative Health Care Management design one such product that is a huge hit with both client organizations and appraisers. Be sure to choose a service that is user-friendly and meets the ANCC requirements for electronic document submission. Along with offering everything listed in the checklist above, CHCM's web-based document solution gives you a customized website that uses your organization's look and branding standards, which gives your documents an exceptionally polished look.

APPENDIX C

ADDITIONAL RESOURCES

Award Websites

American Association of Critical-care Nurses Beacon Award for
Excellence
http://www.aacn.org/wd/beaconapps/content/mainpage.
pcms?menu = beaconapps

ANCC Magnet Recognition Program®
http://www.nursecredentialing.org/Magnet

ANCC Pathway to Excellence®

http://www.nursecredentialing.org/Pathway

Baldrige Performance Excellence Program
http://www.nist.gov/baldrige/

Evidence-Based Practice Resources Websites

ACE Star Model of Knowledge Transformation (Stevens)
http://www.acestar.uthscsa.edu/acestar-model.asp
BMJ Clinical Evidence (subscription required) http://clinical-
evidence.bmj.com/x/index.html

Evidence-Based Nursing journal
http://ebn.bmj.com

Evidence-Based Practice Centers
http://www.ahrq.gov/clinic/epc

The Joanna Briggs Institute for Evidence Based Nursing and Midwifery http://www.joannabriggs.org

NAHRS Task Force on Mapping the Literature of Nursing
http://nahrs.mlanet.org/home/activities/mapnur

National Guideline Clearinghouse
http://www.guideline.gov

National Institute for Nursing Research (NINR)
http://www.ninr.nih.gov/

National Library of Medicine (NLM)
http://www.nlm.nih.gov/

The NICHD Cochrane Neonatal Collaborative Review Group
(alphabetical listing of systematic reviews)
http://www.nichd.nih.gov/cochrane/

Nursing and Allied Health Resources Section
http://nahrs.mlanet.org/

Royal Windsor Society for Nursing Research
http://www.angelfire.com/on/researchnurses/

University of York Health Sciences Research Department
http://www.york.ac.uk/healthsciences/research/

Articles

Kramer, M., Maguire, P., & Schmalenberg, C. (2004). Excellence through evidence. *Journal of Nursing Administration*, *36*(10), 479–491.

Kramer, M., Maguire, P., & Schmalenberg, C. (2010). Nine structures and leadership practices essential for a magnetic (healthy) work environment. *Nursing Administration Quarterly, 34*(1), 4–17.

Kramer, M., & Schmalenberg, C. (2004). Essentials of a magnetic work environment, part 1. *Nursing 2004, 34*(6), 50–54.

Kramer, M., & Schmalenberg, C. (2004). Essentials of a magnetic work environment, part 2. *Nursing 2004, 34*(7), 44–47.

Kramer, M., & Schmalenberg, C. (2004). Essentials of a magnetic work environment, part 3. *Nursing 2004, 34*(8), 44–47.

Kramer, M., & Schmalenberg, C. (2004). Essentials of a magnetic work environment, part 4. *Nursing 2004, 34*(9), 44–48.

Roper, K., & Russell, G. (1997). The effect of peer review on professionalism, autonomy and accountability. *Journal of Nursing Staff Development, 15*(4).

Trinkoff, A., et al. (2010). A comparison of working conditions among nurses in Magnet® and non-Magnet® hospitals. *Journal of Nursing Administration, 40*(7/8), 309–315.

Miscellaneous

Employee motivation resources:

Nelson Motivation, Inc.
Bob Nelson, PhD, is president and a best-selling author of *1001 Ways to Reward Employees*, *The 1001 Rewards and Recognition Fieldbook*, *1001 Ways to Energize Employees*, *1001 Ways to Take Initiative at Work*, and many others. http://www.nelson-motivation.com

Peer review/Talent Management software:
Halogen Software Inc.
http://www.halogensoftware.com

REFERENCES

American Association of Critical-Care Nurses (AACN). (2006, December). *AACN News 23,* 7.

American Association of Critical-Care Nurses (AACN). (2008). Ventilator associated pneumonia. Retrieved from http://www.aacn.org/WD/Practice/Docs/PracticeAlerts/Ventilator%20Associated%20Pneumonia%201-2008.pdf

American Association of Critical-Care Nurses (AACN). (2011a). Are you ready for Beacon? Retrieved from http://www.aacn.org/WD/beaconapps/docs/beacon_audit_tool_2.pdf

American Association of Critical-Care Nurses (AACN). (2011b). "Criteria descriptions." (n.d.) Retrieved from http://www.aacn.org/WD/BeaconApps/Docs/Beacon_Application_Handbook.pdf

American Nurses Association (ANA). (1965). Education for nursing. *American Journal of Nursing, 65*(12), 106–111.

American Nurses Association (ANA). (1978a). *Entry level education for nursing: Its time has come.* Silver Spring, MD: Author.

American Nurses Association (ANA). (1978b). *Peer review.* Silver Spring, MD: Author.

American Nurses Association (ANA). (2010). *SmartBrief reference about motivation.* Silver Spring, MD: Author.

American Nurses Credentialing Center (ANCC). (2013). *2014 Magnet application manual.* Silver Spring, MD: Author.

American Nurses Credentialing Center (ANCC). (2012). *The 2012 Pathway to Excellence application manual.* Silver Spring, MD: Author.

American Nurses Credentialing Center (ANCC). (2008). *The Magnet nursing services recognition program for excellence in nursing service, health care organization, instructions and application process manual.* Washington, DC: Author.

American Nurses Credentialing Center (ANCC). (2014). *Average Magnet® organization characteristics.* Washington DC: Author.

Atkins, S., & Nygaard, J. (2004). Relationship between patient mortality and nurses' level of education. *Journal of the American Medical Association, 291*(11),1320–1321.

Bacon, T. (2006). *What people want: A manager's guide to building relationships that work.* Mountain View, CA: Davies Black Publishing.

Baldrige Performance Excellence Program. (2015). *Baldrige excellence framework (health care): Health care criteria category and item commentary.* Retrieved from http://www.nist.gov/baldrige/publications/upload/2015_2016_Category_and_Item_Commentary_HC.pdf

Barter, M., & McFarland, P. L. (2001). BSN by 2010: A California initiative. *Journal of Nursing Administration, 31*(3), 141–144.

Benner, P., Sutphen, M., Leonard, V., & Day, L. (2010). Educating nurses: A call for radical transformation. *The Carnegie Foundation Report.* San Francisco, CA: Jossey-Bass.

Biro, M. (2013). 5 ways leaders rock employee recognition. *Forbes.com.* Retrieved from http://www.forbes.com/sites/meghanbiro/2013/01/13/5-ways-leaders-rock-employee-recognition/

Briggs, L., Brown, H., Kesten, K., & Heath, J. (2006, December). Certification a benchmark for critical care nursing excellence. *AACN News, 23,* 7. Retrieved from http://ccn.aacnjournals.org/content/26/6/47.full

Bureau of Labor Statistics. (2013). Employment projections 2012–2022. Retrieved from http://www.bls.gov/news.release/ecopro.t08.htm

Centers for Disease Control (CDC). (2015). Retrieved from http://www.cdc.gov/HAI/ca_uti/uti.html

Cipriano, P. (2007). On the record with Pamela Cipriano, editor-in-chief. *American Nurse Today, 2*(4), 26–27.

Cohen, M. (2007). *What you accept is what you teach: Setting standards for employee accountability.* Minneapolis, MN: Creative Health Care Management.

Collins, J. (2001). *Good to great: Why some companies make the leap . . . and others don't.* New York: HarperCollins.

Drenkard, K. (2010). The business case for Magnet®. *Journal of Nursing Administration, 40*(6), 263–271.

Krsek, C. (2011). Investing in nursing retention is a smart move-in today's economy. *American Nurse Review, 6*(4). Retrieved from http://www.americannursetoday.com/investing-in-nursing-retention-is-a-smart-move-in-todays-economy/

Felgen, J. (2007). *I₂E₂: Leading lasting change.* Minneapolis, MN: Creative Health Care Management.

Gordon, S. (2002). *From silence to voice: What nurses know and must communicate to the public.* (2nd ed.). Ithaca, NY: Cornell University Press.

Guanci, G. (2005). Destination Magnet: Charting a course to excellence. *Journal for Nurses in Staff Development, 21*(5), 227–235.

Guanci, G. (2007). Staff development story: Tips for a successful Magnet journey. *Journal for Nurses in Staff Development, 23*(2), 89–94.

Hersey, P., & Blanchard, K. (1996). *Management of organizational behavior* (10th ed.). Upper Saddle River, New Jersey: Prentice Hall.

Institute of Medicine (IOM). (2010). The future of nursing lead-
    ing change, advancing health. Retrieved from http://iom.
    nationalacademies.org/Reports/2010/The-Future-of-Nursing-
    Leading-Change-Advancing-Health.aspx

Karkos, B., & Peters, K. A. (2007). Magnet community hospital:
    Fewer barriers to nursing research utilization. *JONA*, *36*(7–8),
    377–382.

Koloroutis, M. (Ed.). (2004). *Relationship-Based Care: A model for
    transforming practice*. Minneapolis, MN: Creative Health Care
    Management.

Kramer, M. (2003). Magnet hospital nurses describe control over
    nursing practice. *Western Journal of Nursing Research*, *25*(4),
    434–452.

Kutney-Lee, A., Stimpfel, A., Sloane, D., Cimiotti, J., Quinn, L., &
    Aiken, L. (2015). Changes in patient and nurse outcomes asso-
    ciated with magnet hospital recognition. *Medical Care*, *53*(6),
    550–557.

Lower, J. (2007). Utilizing peer reviews. *Advance for Nurses*.
    Retrieved from http://nursing.advanceweb.com/common/Edi-
    torial/printfriendly.aspx?cc=68322

Manojlovich, M. (2007). Power and empowerment in nursing:
    Looking backward to inform the future. *The Online Journal of
    Issues in Nursing*, *12*(1). Retrieved from http://www.nursing-
    world.org/MainMenuCategories/ANAMarketplace/ANA-
    Periodicals/OJIN/TableofContents/Volume122007/No1Jan07/
    LookingBackwardtoInformtheFuture.aspx

Manthey, M., & Miller, D. (1994). Empowerment through levels of
    authority. *Journal of Nursing Administration*, *24* (7–8), 23.

McClure, M., & Hinshaw, A. S. (Eds.). (2002). *Magnet hospitals
    revisited: Attraction and retention of professional nurses*. Washing-
    ton, DC: American Nurses Publishing.

McCormick, M. (1990). *Success secrets*. Waukegan, IL: Fontana Press.

Meade, C., Bursell, A., & Ketelsen, L. (2006). Effects of nursing rounds on patients' call light use, satisfaction, and safety. *American Journal of Nursing, 106*(9), 58–70.

National Institute of Standards and Technology (NIST). (2015). Malcolm Baldrige National Quality Award application data—1988–2015. Retrieved from http://www.nist.gov/public_affairs/factsheet/nqa_appdata.cfm

National Institute of Standards and Technology (NIST). (2011a). Are we making progress? Retrieved from http://www.nist.gov/baldrige/publications/progress.cfm

National Institute of Standards and Technology (NIST). (2011b). Are we making progress as leaders? Retrieved from http://www.nist.gov/baldrige/publications/progress_leaders.cfm

Nelson, R. (1999). The ten ironies of motivation. *Workforce Management.* Retrieved from http://www.workforce.com/articles/the-ten-ironies-of-motivation.

Nelson, R. (2005). *1001 ways to reward employees.* New York: Workman Publishing.

Nightingale, F. (1860). *Notes on nursing* (1st American ed.). New York: D. Appleton & Company.

Pixar Animation Studios (Producer), & Lasseter, J. (Director). (1995). *Toy Story* (motion picture). U.S: Pixar Animation Studios.

Porter-O'Grady, T. (2003). Researching shared governance—A futility of focus. *Journal of Nursing Administration, 33*(4), 251–252.

Schein, E. (2004). *Organizational culture and leadership* (3rd ed.). San Francisco: Jossey-Bass.

Stevens, K. R. (2012). *ACE Star Model of EBP: Knowledge transformation.* Academic Center for Evidence-based Practice. The University of Texas Health Science Center at San Antonio.

Surviving Sepsis Campaign. (2015). SSC six-hour bundle revised. Retrieved from http://www.survivingsepsis.org/News/Pages/SSC-Six-Hour-Bundle-Revised.aspx

Swihart, D. (2006). *Shared governance: A practical approach to reshaping professional nursing practice*. Marblehead, MA: HC Pro.

University of Minnesota School of Nursing. (2000). Evidence based nursing. Retrieved from http://hsl.lib.umn.edu/learn/ebp/mod01/index.html

Wikipedia. Business Proposal. (2015a). In *Wikipedia*. Retrieved from https://en.wikipedia.org/wiki/Proposal_(business)

Wikipedia. (2015b). Excellence. Retrieved from http://en.wikipedia.org/wiki/Excellence

Wikipedia. (2015c). Institutional review board. Retrieved from http://en.wikipedia.org/wiki/Institutional_Review_Board

Wolf, G. A., & Greenhouse, P. K. (2007). Blueprint for design: Creating models that direct change. *Journal of Nursing Administration*, *37*(9), 381–387.

Yoder-Wise, P. (1999). *Leading and managing in nursing* (2nd ed.). St Louis, MO: Mosby.

YourDictionary. (2015). Empowerment. Retrieved from http://www.yourdictionary.com/empowerment#wiktionary

YourDictionary. (2015) Excellence. Retrieved from http://www.yourdictionary.com/excellence

ABOUT THE AUTHOR

Gen Guanci is uncompromisingly focused on advancing nursing as a profession and on nursing professional development. Whether she's guiding organizations as they establish a Culture of Excellence, including the journey to Magnet® designation, educating on Relationship-Based Care, or helping education departments strengthen structures, processes, and outcomes, she sees the possibilities in everyone with whom she is honored to work.

Gen has a master's degree in education and a certificate of advanced graduate studies (CAGS) in Organization Development from Cambridge College in Cambridge, Massachusetts. She is certified in critical care nursing (CCRN-K), as well as in nursing professional development (RN-BC). Gen has served as an officer of the Association of Nursing Professional Development (ANPD), formerly the National Nursing Staff Development Organization (NNSDO), and is past president of the ANPD Affiliate–North Eastern Organization of Nurse Educators

(NEONE). She is a past multiyear invited member of the National Magnet® Conference Continuing Education Task Force, which is responsible for the selection of conference presentations and posters.

One of Gen's great strengths is her breadth of knowledge. She has lived and worked internationally, giving her a keen familiarity with a variety of health care systems, and she's worked with nurses educated all over the world. She also brings her far-ranging background to each job, seamlessly blending Relationship-Based Care with her expertise in creating a culture of excellence and creating customized structures and processes tailored to measure specific outcomes. Gen prides herself on her ability to take complex and detailed subjects and make them easily understood.

For additional information on what Gen or Creative Health Care Management can do for your organization, please contact her at 800.728.7766 ext. 213 or via email at gguanci@chcm.com.

ORDER FORM

1. Order Online at shop.chcm.com.
2. Call toll-free 800.728.7766 ext. 4 and use your Visa, Mastercard, Amex or Discover or a company purchase order.
3. Fax your order to: 952.854.1866.
4. Mail your order with pre-payment or company purchase order to:

   Creative Health Care Management
   5610 Rowland Road, Suite 100
   Minneapolis, MN 55343
   Attn: Resources Department

CREATIVE

HEALTH CARE

MANAGEMENT

Product	Price	Quantity	Subtotal	TOTAL
B675—*Feel the Pull*	$24.95			
B510—*Relationship-Based Care: A Model for Transforming Practice*	$34.95			
B558—*What You Accept Is What You Teach*	$16.00			
B560—I_2E_2: *Leading Lasting Change*	$24.95			
B605—*Time to Lead*	$19.95			
Shipping Costs: Please call 800.728.7766 x4 for a shipping estimate.				
Order TOTAL				

Need more than one copy? We have quantity discounts available.

Quantity Discounts (Books Only)		
10–49 = *10% off*	50–99 = *20% off*	100 or more = *30% off*

Payment Methods: ☐ Credit Card　　☐ Check　　☐ Purchase Order PO# _____

Credit Card	Number			Expiration	AVS (3 digits)
Visa / Mastercard / Amex / Discover	—	—	—	/	
Cardholder address (if different from below):	Signature:				

Customer Information	
Name:	
Title:	
Company:	
Address:	
City, State, Zip:	
Daytime Phone:	
Email:	

Satisfaction guarantee: If you are not satisfied with your purchase, simply return the products within 30 days for a full refund.
For a free catalog of all our products, visit www.chcm.com or call 800.728.7766 ext. 4.

Cultures of Excellence

CREATING A CULTURE OF EXCELLENCE

In today's health care environment of staffing shortages and high customer expectations, organizations need to attract and retain quality employees while supporting professional nursing practice and enhancing patient outcomes.

Creative Health Care Management has a proven track record of guiding organizations along the journey to organizational and nursing excellence, whether they are applying for formal award designation (including ANCC Magnet® recognition) or creating their own Cultures of Excellence. We provide the inspiration, infrastructure, education, and evidence for each step in creating a Culture of Excellence through the following services:

- Journey to Excellence Support
- Organizational Assessment using the 2014 Magnet® Model
- Shared Governance/Decision Making Support
- Professional Practice Model, Framework and Care Delivery Model Design
- Professional Advancement Programs (Clinical Ladders)
- Effective Peer Review and Feedback
- Evidence-Based Practice and Nursing Research
- Using Outcomes to Drive Practice
- Cultures of Excellence Workshops
- Magnet Document Services

And MORE!

CLIENT FEEDBACK

CHCM puts an emphasis on developing a relationship with you and your organization. They invest their heart and soul.
—Pamela Lundy, Director of Resource Management and Special Projects, Susquehanna Health System

In working with Gen, I got a master's class in Magnet preparation.
—Susan Santana, Director of Professional Practice, Lowell General Hospital

There is not a Gen Guanci around every corner—that knowledgeable nurturing/mentoring/teaching spirit. I tell other Magnet® program directors about Gen every chance I get.
—Susan Crandall, Magnet® Program Co-Manager

The whole organization reacted well to Gen. She inspired confidence. When she said, "let's do this or that," it wasn't like it was something we'd just try. If Gen recommended it, we knew it would actually work.
—Susan Santana, Director of Professional Practice, Lowell General Hospital

The most valuable thing is Creative Health Care
Management's expansive knowledge and connections.
They have the latest and greatest intel about what
other hospitals are doing.
—MARGAUX CHAN, MAGNET® PROGRAM MANAGER,
CHILDREN'S HOSPITAL LOS ANGELES

Gen was very honest and willing to give us "hard" news
if it meant helping us accomplish our Magnet® goal. Her
honesty was an important thing.
—DEBBIE OWENS, MSN RN NE-BC, MAGNET®
PROGRAM DIRECTOR, ST. VINCENT'S MEDICAL CENTER

People ask me about the cost of working with CHCM. I
tell them, "I'm a tough person. I don't spend my money
foolishly. I've always gotten a return on investment, and
I'm investing on behalf of patients, families and staff."
—KATHLEEN VANWAGONER, FORMER CHIEF NURSING
OFFICER, CRITTENTON HOSPITAL MEDICAL CENTER